MATT CHRISTOPHER®

At the Plate with...
Ken Griffey Jr.

MATT CHRISTOPHER®

At the Plate with . . .
Ken Griffey Jr.

Text by Glenn Stout

LITTLE, BROWN AND COMPANY
New York ॐ An AOL Time Warner Company

First Edition

Matt Christopher® is a registered trademark of
Catherine M. Christopher

Cover photograph by David L. Kyle, Sports Illustrated / © Time Inc.

Library of Congress Cataloging-in-Publication Data

Stout, Glenn.
    Ken Griffey Jr. /Glenn Stout. — 1st ed.
       p. cm.
    Summary: Discusses the professional and personal life of the baseball star who plays with the Seattle Mariners.
    ISBN 0-316-14233-6
    1. Griffey, Ken, Jr. — Juvenile literature. 2.   Baseball players — United States — Biography — Juvenile literature. [1. Griffey, Ken Jr. 2. Baseball players. 3. Afro-Americans — Biography.]
I. Title.
GV865.G69C47   1997
796.357'092
[B]—dc20   96-40974

10 9 8 7

COM-MO

Printed in the United States of America

Contents

Prologue

The noise of the crowd was earsplitting. It shook the entire stadium. The Yankee pitcher stared at the signal from his catcher, then began his windup. At the plate, in the left-handed batter's box, stood the Seattle hitter — tall and muscular, with the face of a kid. The Yankee pitcher let the ball fly.

The eyes of the "kid" fastened on the baseball. His hands tightened on the bat handle. His right foot lifted off the ground, hips pivoting as he brought the bat forward in a long, looping arc. . . .

Crack! The sound split the air. It was louder than the crowd's rumbling roar. The ball rose higher and higher, disappearing against the gray roof of the Seattle Kingdome stadium. The Yankee right fielder looked up helplessly as the ball landed in the upper deck.

The "kid" at the plate watched it go as he trotted down the first base line. Then he flashed the smile that has made him world famous. The smile that seems to say "I love this game." The smile that has made his face — Ken Griffey Jr.'s face — the face of baseball.

In the stands that October night in 1995 were thousands of kids, and millions more were watching the game on TV. All of them, even the Yankee fans, loved Ken Griffey Jr.

Any kid who has ever loved the game of baseball can't help admiring "Junior." His skills are amazing, but it is his joy in playing that reminds fans what the game of baseball is really all about: fun.

Ken Griffey Jr. has been having fun on the base-ball field since he was just a toddler. His father, Ken Griffey Sr., was a fine major league player himself. In fact, baseball talent in the Griffey family goes back even further than that.

Chapter One
1969–1981

Ken Griffey Sr.'s Son

The little town of Donora, Pennsylvania, had already produced one baseball great — Hall of Famer Stan "the Man" Musial. One of the people Musial played with on the Donora High School team was left-handed third baseman, Buddy Griffey.

Buddy was a high school baseball star. But in the 1940s, blacks were not allowed to play baseball in the major leagues. They had to play in the separate Negro Leagues. Buddy Griffey didn't make it that far, though. He had a wife and six children to take care of by the time he reached his midtwenties. One day, the strain of supporting them proved to be too much for him. When his son Ken was only two years old, Buddy left the family.

George Kenneth Griffey Sr. was born on April 10, 1950. After his father left, his mother, Ruth, had to struggle to bring up her children. She worked at odd jobs and sometimes had to accept welfare. Ken did see his father again — seven years later — but they were strangers by then, and they have never been close since.

During his high school years, Ken worked after school to help make ends meet. The state Youth Corps gave him a job paying $65.10 every two weeks. With all his jobs, however, Ken still managed to find time for sports. At Donora High, he starred in football, baseball, and track.

Baseball was not even his best sport! Still, a scout from the Cincinnati Reds thought he had potential. By this time, Jackie Robinson had broken the color barrier, and African Americans were playing in the major leagues. In the 1969 baseball draft, the Reds picked Griffey in the twenty-ninth round, and he began working his way up through their minor league farm system.

His talent aside, Ken was a friendly boy, and girls liked him. One year, the school held a dance for Sadie Hawkins Day — the day girls traditionally ask boys out. One girl wanted to invite Ken to the dance, but she was too shy, so she asked her friend Alberta to do it for her. Bertie, as Alberta's friends called her, was more outgoing and strong willed than her shy friend. She was also an athlete, like Ken. She played both basketball and volleyball.

When Alberta asked Ken to go to the dance with her friend, he said no. "Then will you go with me?" she boldly asked. "Yes," Ken replied with a smile. Bertie's friend never spoke to her again. But Bertie didn't care, because she had made up her mind that Ken Griffey was the man for her.

While they were still in high school, Ken and Alberta got married. The year Ken was drafted by the Cincinnati Reds, they had a child on the way. That child turned out to be the great Ken Griffey Jr. Junior was born on November 21, 1969, in Donora. By the age of seven months, he was already walking. Ken and Alberta thought it was a sign that Junior might have athletic ability. Little did they know how right they were!

By this time, Ken Sr. was playing in the minor leagues. He had high hopes for the future but still had a long way to go before getting a chance to play in the majors.

Two years later, the Griffeys had another son,

Craig. Ken Sr. traveled a lot in the next years, working his way up through the minors. And everywhere he went, he brought his young and growing family with him. He swore to himself that he would never leave his wife and children behind the way his father had left him. Whatever happened, he was going to be a father to his sons. So wherever he played, there in the stands sat little Ken and Craig Griffey. The ballparks were their playground, and both boys decided then and there that they would become professional baseball players, like their dad.

While Ken Sr. was working his way up through the Reds' minor league farm system, the family did not have much money. In those days, even major league stars did not make anything like what today's average player makes. And minor leaguers have never made much money. They play because their dream is to make it to the big leagues.

In the off-seasons, Ken Sr. would take other jobs in Donora to help support his family. Once or twice, when work was not available, he even had to rely on government welfare checks, as his mother once had.

But Ken Sr. was determined to make it to the majors. He practiced his baseball skills endlessly. And the hard work paid off. Every year he improved, and slowly he made his way up the minor league ladder from Rookie League, to A ball, to Double A, and then Triple A. Finally, in 1973, the call from the majors came. The Cincinnati Reds wanted him to join them!

As always, Ken Sr. brought his family along with him. The four Griffeys arrived in Cincinnati happy and excited about the future. That season, Ken Sr. played in twenty-five games for the team that would soon become known as "the Big Red Machine."

The Reds' second baseman was Joe Morgan. The catcher was Johnny Bench. The shortstop was Dave Concepcion. At first base, and sometimes third, was Tony Perez. Also on the team were George Foster, Cesar Geronimo, and Pete Rose, who would collect more hits in his career than any player in the history of baseball. Their manager was the great Sparky Anderson.

For Ken Jr., now four years old, these tremendous players were just "the men Daddy works with." He knew from the size of the stadium and the crowds that this was different from the minor leagues, but he was still too young to appreciate that his father was now a major leaguer.

Kenny often came to Cincinnati's Riverfront Stadium to see his father play. There he'd romp with the sons of the other players: Eduardo and Victor Perez, Pete Rose Jr., Lee May Jr., and Brian McRae. The youngsters were wild. During practices and before games, they would run around the ballpark and the locker rooms like madmen. Sparky Anderson remembers Ken Jr. raiding his dugout refrigerator and helping himself to sodas. But everyone agreed that they were good kids — and they all showed athletic talent. The players even nicknamed them "the Little Red Machine."

Ken Griffey Sr. played in eighty-eight games for the Reds during the 1974 season. He soon became a fixture in right field and a rising young star. In 1975 he batted .305, and the Reds won the World Series.

The next year was even better — Griffey Sr. hit .336, and the Big Red Machine became a dynasty, winning the World Series for the second time in a row. Griffey Sr. also stole thirty-four bases that year. At five feet eleven inches tall and 190 pounds, he wasn't a power hitter, but he hit for a high average (.296) his whole career. He also had great speed and excellent defensive skills, making him a top-notch all-around player.

Of course, to Ken Jr., Number 30 on the Reds wasn't a famous baseball star — he was just "Dad." Having grown up around ballparks, Junior didn't realize how special his father's accomplishments were. That is, until the 1980 All-Star game.

In that game, Griffey Sr. hit a home run and was named the game's Most Valuable Player (MVP). Finally, ten-year-old Junior was impressed. He realized that his dad was somebody special, not just to him but to millions of baseball fans all over the country.

By that time, Junior had been playing baseball for a few years himself. At age seven, he was already throwing the ball around in the backyard with his dad. At eight, he entered Little League. There, Junior was an instant sensation. He pitched and played outfield for the Mount Airy D1 team. As pitcher, he won twelve games without a single loss. And to top it off, he batted 1.000 his first season — getting a hit every time he came up to the plate!

Ken Sr. was bursting with pride at his son's athletic ability. "Remember — no one is better than you are," he told him. Those words must have stuck in Junior's mind, because he has played with amazing confidence ever since.

Of course, no one can ever be perfect, and no ballplayer can go on forever without making an out. His second season in Little League, Junior did something that he thought he would never do — he struck out! Devastated, he stormed away from home plate, close to tears. Afterward, his mother had to remind him that even his father sometimes struck out.

Ken Jr.'s childhood might sound like heaven to some people: growing up at the ballpark, with all those famous players around. But being the son of a famous athlete comes with a price — as Junior soon found out.

Chapter Two
1981–1987

Teen Phenom

In 1981, after many great seasons with Cincinnati, Ken Griffey Sr. was traded to the New York Yankees. That meant he would have to leave Cincinnati.

By this time, Ken Jr. and his little brother, Craig, were both in school. They were in Little League, too, with friends of their own, a new little sister, and a nice home. Whenever he had moved before, Ken Sr. had taken his family with him. This time, the decision was made that the family would stay behind in Cincinnati.

The separation was not an easy one. Ken Jr. didn't see much of his father anymore, except in the winters, and he missed his dad terribly. The two of them would speak over the phone frequently. Whenever Junior had a problem, he would wait till late that night, after the Yankee game was over, then phone New York long-distance to talk to his dad.

The timing of Griffey Sr.'s move to New York could hardly have been worse: At twelve years old, just on the verge of becoming a teenager, Junior needed his dad more than ever.

Junior began to misbehave, hitting his brother and a boy at school. When his father heard about it, he summoned Ken Jr. to New York. Junior was afraid he was going to get "whupped," but his dad surprised him by bringing him to Yankee Stadium instead. "You wanna hit?" he asked his son. "Fine. You can hit." And he proceeded to take him out onto the field and throw him batting practice.

After that, Junior would act up once in a while just so he could go to New York. Each time, his dad would take him to the ballpark early and throw Junior some batting practice. At first, Junior missed as many pitches as he hit. But he was getting taller and stronger every month. Soon, his dad could no longer strike him out.

On these visits, Griffey Sr. would coach his son, too, giving him tips that he could take home and use to improve his game. These frequent coaching sessions helped make Junior the ballplayer he has become.

Today, Ken Griffey Jr. readily admits that his father spoiled him. Alberta Griffey agrees, and Ken Sr. doesn't argue with her. "I didn't mind spoiling him," he says. Remembering his own father, he adds, "A lot of things Junior did, I didn't get a chance to do when I was that age. I wanted him and Craig to have what I couldn't."

Meanwhile, back at home in Little League, Junior was continuing to improve at baseball. By the time he was fourteen, he was able to hit the ball 400 feet — farther than some major leaguers! He was a terrific outfielder, too. He played very shallow, but he was so fast and got such a good jump on the ball that it was rare to see one go over his head. In fact, Junior still plays a shallow center field, saying that he goes back on balls better than he comes in.

With his speed, his power, and his obvious athletic ability, Ken Griffey Jr. was already beginning to attract attention from major league scouts. But during this time, his dad rarely got to see him play. And the funny thing was, whenever Ken Sr. did show up, Junior never managed to play very well.

In fact, he got a total of exactly one hit in all his times at bat in front of his father!

Was it the pressure of having his dad in the stands? Definitely, Junior admits. "When he was there, it was the only time I thought I had to impress somebody." Then, with a smile, he remembers what his father would tell him after those awful games. "He'd say he was the one guy I *didn't* have to impress. As long as I was happy with what I was doing, he didn't care if I was a garbageman or whatever."

Ken Sr. managed to see only seven or eight of his son's games over those years. But when he was in town, the two would spend lots of time together, tossing the baseball around or playing one-on-one basketball. During one such game, when he was fourteen, Junior finally managed to block one of his father's shots. Griffey Sr. put down the basketball and said, "That's it. I quit." Junior was astonished and didn't understand. But the father had seen what the son could not: that the time was fast approaching when Ken Griffey Jr. would come into his own. The time for childhood games was over.

Ken Griffey Jr. entered Moeller Senior High

14

School the following September. By now, he had become a superb athlete, and he immediately joined Moeller's varsity squads in both baseball and football. He played football just as well as he did baseball — maybe even better. His father was almost always away during the baseball season, but he did manage to see most of Junior's football games.

Then, suddenly, Junior got some shocking news. Because he was doing poorly in his classes, school policy said he could not participate in athletics. He was taken off both teams! Ken's grades had gone down as he spent more and more time on the athletic field. It was not the first time he'd had this kind of trouble. Once, when he was twelve, his mother had benched him for a whole week for doing poorly in school.

At first, Ken was devastated. He wanted so badly to be out on the field, helping his teammates win a championship. But he soon realized that there was only one thing he could do to get back on the teams — study.

Ever since he'd been a toddler, Ken Jr. had loved a challenge. Now, he hit the books as if they were defensive linemen. He brought his grades back up by sheer hard work and determination. By the time his junior year came around, he had done it. He was back on both teams.

When fall came, and football season rolled around again, he starred at tailback for the Moeller team, wearing number 36. He also played at wide receiver, punter, and placekicker. Watching him, many fans, including his dad, thought he might have a future in the National Football League. But Junior had other dreams.

Ever since he was fourteen years old, professional baseball scouts had been watching Ken Griffey Jr. But the scout who knew him best, who had seen him play the most, was his own mother, Alberta Griffey. She had seen him progress, year after year. The summer he was sixteen, she decided Ken Jr. was ready to join the Connie Mack baseball league.

The Connie Mack League was for teens of exceptional baseball talent from around the country. Their games were watched by lots of pro scouts. Alberta Griffey did not have an easy time convincing her husband that their son was good enough for Connie Mack baseball. Whenever Ken Sr. had seen his son play, Junior had done a lot of striking out.

Besides, Junior was only sixteen years old. In Connie Mack ball, he'd be playing against eighteen-year-olds. It took Alberta three months to convince her husband, but she stuck to her guns. She believed so much in her son's abilities that she refused to give in.

And did she ever turn out to be right. Not only did Junior play well in Connie Mack baseball, he led his team, the Midland Cardinals, to the league's world series, where he hit three home runs — one to each part of the outfield!

That year, he starred for Moeller's baseball team, too. Batting third in the order, he hit 10 home runs, with a .478 average in twenty-eight games. He drove in 33 runs and made just two errors in center field. He was voted Player of the Year.

At the end of Ken's junior year, his dad told him it was time for him to choose between football and baseball. Ken Sr. felt that his son could not continue to play both sports and hope to go all the way to the top in one of them. In the fall of his senior year, Ken Jr. made his decision. He quit the football team, to the surprise of everyone but his mother. She had known all along that her son's real dream was to play baseball, like his dad.

"All he talked about was playing baseball," Ken Sr. said later, remembering those days with wonder. "I wanted him to play football, but it was his decision. He had all those scouts watching him."

Junior may have had trouble hitting in front of his father, but he did just fine when the pro scouts were around. They were all talking about him now, as he starred again in his senior season at Moeller. That year, he hit .478 again, with 7 homers and 23 runs batted in (RBIs). For the second time in a row, he was made Player of the Year!

He was a lefty hitter, like Ken Sr. But he was taller than his father — six foot three — and bigger — 195 pounds — and he hit for more power, with a long, looping swing that was still somehow completely in control. It was a beautiful swing to watch — many since then have called it a perfect swing.

Ken played the field beautifully, too, running down balls no one else could ever have caught, diving recklessly to make stupendous "circus catches" — the kind of plays that seem impossible. His father had been an excellent fielder, too, but Ken Jr. had a grace in the outfield that not even his dad

18

could match. Both had good speed and cannons for arms. And both played the game with heart and with great joy.

The Griffeys were rightly proud of their son, but even they were astounded by what happened on June 2, 1987. Just before his high school graduation, Ken Jr. got some incredible news — the Seattle Mariners had chosen him as the first pick overall in the baseball amateur draft! He was only seventeen years old. He had always dreamed of being a professional baseball player. Now, that dream was about to become reality.

Chapter Three
1987–1988

A Difficult Season

Ken Griffey Jr. hadn't realized until that spring that you could get drafted into the pros right after high school. He'd figured on going to college first and playing baseball there before entering the minor leagues. But destiny was calling, and Junior felt the pull. A few days after graduating from Moeller, he signed his Mariners contract.

There was never any doubt in his mind about signing. The Mariners were offering him a signing bonus of $160,000! Back in 1969, when his dad had first signed with the Cincinnati Reds, there hadn't been any bonus at all. True, Ken Sr. had been drafted in the twenty-ninth round, but even for top picks in those days, bonuses weren't nearly that high.

Nevertheless, Junior read over his contract carefully and had lawyers look at it, too. Back when he'd made his choice of baseball over football, his mom had warned him that if he chose baseball, he'd better learn how to read a contract, "because one word can change everything." Ken Jr. took her advice to heart.

Junior was assigned to the Mariners' Rookie League team in Bellingham, Washington. The Bellingham team played in the Northwest League, which was a good league for young players to start out in. They played a short season, giving the players a chance to adjust gradually to the life of a professional ballplayer.

But not everything about going to Bellingham was good. For one thing, the state of Washington was halfway across the country from Cincinnati, Ohio. Junior had been away for a few nights at a time during his travels in the Connie Mack League, but now he would be separated from his family for months! Kenny was only seventeen, and he wasn't sure he was ready to be so far away for so long.

It was hard leaving home. Junior packed his bags and boarded the plane as full of anxieties as of hopes. Would he play well? Would he get along with the other players and his coaches? He knew he would be homesick, but he figured he could always make a lot of phone calls. That was how he and his dad had stayed in touch during Ken Sr.'s long absences during the baseball season.

Still, Kenny was not prepared for Bellingham. A small town north of Seattle, near the border of Canada, it was a very different place from Cincinnati. Junior was used to the big city. And there weren't very many African Americans in Bellingham. He felt strange, as if he stood out here. It had been only two weeks since his high school graduation, and here he was in a different world!

But fans in Bellingham greeted him like a hero. They had heard all about his high school exploits, and, of course, his father was the famous Ken Griffey. All eyes were on Junior the first time he trotted onto the field.

He didn't disappoint the Bellingham fans. His very first hit, on July 17, 1987, was a home run against Everett.

That first week, he hit 3 homers, stole 4 bases, and drove in 8 runs. He was voted Northwest League Player of the Week. Every time he stepped up to the plate, wearing his number 24 uniform, the announcer at the ballpark would ask the fans, "What time is it?" "Griffey time!" they would all shout back.

But all was not as well as it appeared. Kenny was having trouble adjusting. He felt uncomfortable in Bellingham. He missed his home, his family, and his friends. He had so much on his mind that he twice got picked off first base. His manager, Rick Sweet, lectured him, saying, "You can't be a spectator when you're out there playing the game!"

Junior knew that being a professional ballplayer was going to take some getting used to. He was here to mature and to improve, and it was going to take time. Still, as the weeks went by, the stress began to take its toll. Ken went into a slump at the plate that he just couldn't seem to get out of. His batting average fell all the way to .230. For the first time since he'd started playing baseball, he wasn't having fun.

Off the field, things weren't so great either. The team traveled around in an ancient bus built in 1958. It had no air-conditioning, no bathroom, and the seats were all ripped, with stuffing coming out of them. The team spent many hours at a time on the bus, traveling from town to town. When he was playing for Moeller High, and even in the Connie Mack League, the traveling conditions had been much better. And of course, Junior had spent a lot of time in the major league ballparks. The difference in conditions of the parks, clubhouses, and dugouts was a bit of a shock to him.

Even worse, the bus driver's two teenage sons kept taunting him because of the color of his skin. They called him horrible names, and even threatened to get a gun and come after him. Kenny was hurt, scared, and upset. He had never encountered this kind of vicious prejudice before. No wonder he was distracted on the ball field!

To make matters worse, Junior didn't feel close enough to anyone in Bellingham to talk about his problems. So he called home every night, running up huge phone bills as his homesickness grew every day. He began to think seriously about quitting. Maybe he wasn't cut out for this life after all, he told his mother and his girlfriend. He told them he was thinking of packing it in and coming back home.

But Alberta Griffey reminded him of who he was. He was a winner, not a quitter. He just had to concentrate more on his game. His girlfriend told him that although she missed him terribly, she wanted him to stick it out in Bellingham.

He did stick it out, but it was far from easy. He began to stay out late at night, well past the team curfew. When he was caught, the manager benched him for a couple of games.

It was during this time that his mother came to visit him. Because she cared so much about him, she leveled with him. "You'll never make it if you keep fooling around. Get your head together and turn your game around, Junior!" she warned. By the time she went back to Cincinnati, Kenny was determined to follow her advice.

He began to play better almost at once. Then, on July 4, going after a long fly ball with his usual reckless abandon, he crashed into the center field wall and injured his shoulder. At first, Kenny was afraid it might be the end of his season. So he was relieved when the team doctor told him he'd only have to miss a week. Kenny decided to use that week to get himself mentally ready to play. He promised himself that never again would he allow any off-the-field problems to distract him.

When he got back into action on July 12, he was

a changed man. He played as if he were on a mission. For the next month, he hit .453 with 7 more homers and 16 RBIs!

By the end of the season, Junior had impressed everyone with his turnaround and comeback. His season numbers were .320 batting average, 40 RBIs, 14 home runs, and 13 stolen bases. He was voted onto the All-League team. The magazine *Baseball America* named him the top major league prospect in the Northwest League.

It was a sweet end of the season for Junior, but his happiness turned sour soon after. He found out that he wouldn't be going directly home for the offseason. The Northwest League played a short season, and the Mariners wanted Ken to go down to the Arizona Instructional League for the rest of the fall, to sharpen his fundamental baseball skills.

Junior soon found himself in another strange place, forced to adjust yet again. And all the while, he was being lectured to and yelled at by his coaches. It stung to be yelled at. Kenny was not used to it. Back at Moeller, and in Connie Mack League, the coaches had encouraged him and let him play his game. Here in the pros, it was different.

When he finally came home that fall, Kenny was feeling moody, upset, and rebellious. He had been the victim of racial prejudice. He had gone through his first long hitting slump. He had been injured for the first time. He had been lonely and depressed. Strangers had yelled at him when he couldn't match their giant expectations.

At home, too, things were different. There was a growing friction between him and his father. Ken Sr. didn't like the way his son moped around all day and stayed out late at night. He wanted Junior to start being a responsible man, not a boy who needed prodding. He told Junior that the time had come to start paying rent or to get his own place.

They fought almost every day, and neither one could totally understand why. They had always been friends as well as father and son. What was going on?

The truth was, Ken Jr. was having a crisis. For the first time in his life, he was deeply unhappy. He wondered if he'd ever make it in baseball the way his dad had. If he was so good, why was everyone always yelling at him?

He even thought about suicide. And one terrible

day, he actually tried it. While his friends struggled to stop him, he grabbed a bottle of aspirin and emptied it down his throat. He swallowed 277 tablets and wound up in the emergency room of Providence Hospital, in Mount Airy, Ohio. The doctors there pumped out his stomach.

When Ken Sr. heard what had happened, he rushed to the hospital. He found Junior in the intensive care unit, resting on a bed with IV tubes in his arms. Ken Sr. was so scared for his son that his fear came out in anger. He immediately started to yell at Junior. Junior sat up and, without a word, ripped the tubes out of his arms.

Finally, his father understood. It was the yelling itself that had so upset his son. He fell silent, and the two men exchanged looks of deep understanding. From that moment on, their relationship was transformed.

Ken Sr. and Ken Jr. became closer than ever before. They spent a lot of time together that winter, talking baseball, talking about what it means to be a man. There was no more yelling; there were no more fights. Father and son had become a team. Nothing could stop them now.

Chapter Four
1988

On the Rise Again

When spring came around, Junior departed for the Mariners' spring training camp. He was excited at the prospect of wearing a Mariners uniform for the first time and hanging out with the major leaguers — even if it was only for a couple of weeks.

Junior knew he was not going to be in the majors that season. The Mariners were sending him to San Bernardino, California, to join their California A League team, the Spirit. The move was a promotion, and Junior meant to make the most of his opportunity.

Ken Sr. promised to come see him play when the Atlanta Braves, his current team, came to nearby Los Angeles to play the Dodgers. The two men shook hands and hugged, and Junior boarded his plane.

He was eighteen now — still young, but more mature after his crisis. For the moment, the Griffey family decided to say nothing publicly about his suicide attempt. There would be time for that later, when talking about it wouldn't endanger his career. Junior finally did tell the newspapers about it four years later, when he was already a star for the Mariners. Even then, talking about his crisis was not easy for him.

"I got depressed. I got angry. I didn't want to live," he told reporters. "But I'm talking about it now because I want young people to know how wrong and how foolish it was to try suicide." He hoped his story would encourage young people in crisis to get help before it was too late. "Suicide," he said, "is not the solution."

He also made it clear that he would never talk about the incident again. That time in his life was past, and he had put it behind him.

That season, in San Bernardino, Ken Griffey Jr. came of age. He left his doubts behind him and played with supreme confidence. By the time his dad made it out to Fiscalini Field that April to see him play, Junior was ready. He had never played well in front of his father. On this night, he was determined to change that.

It was only the beginning of the season, but Junior was on fire, hitting .520, with 4 homers and 11 RBIs. The Spirit were 7–0, while Ken Sr.'s Atlanta Braves were in last place with an 0–10 record. Ken Sr. was slumping badly, hitting just .091. Before the game, Junior ribbed him about it, offering to give him some pointers.

In the first inning, Junior came up to bat. Determined to finally get a hit in front of his dad, he bunted down the third base line. The fielders were stunned; they never expected a power hitter like Griffey to bunt! Junior reached first base easily and grinned at his father. Ken Sr. laughed out loud and shook his head.

By the time the eighth inning rolled around, Junior had made several great plays in the field and singled home two runs. Now he came to the plate again, swinging the bat his dad had brought him that day. Facing a 3–2 count, he took an outside fastball and hit it sky-high, out over the fence, past the trees behind the stadium. As the ball disappeared in the distance, well over 400 feet from home plate,

Griffey Sr., a guest in the broadcast booth, sat with his hand over his mouth, shocked at his son's power. "Did you see how far that ball went?" he asked the radio announcer.

Junior rounded the bases, pointing his finger at his father and grinning from ear to ear. That night, Ken Sr. called Alberta and told her what he had seen. Junior had impressed him in all five areas of baseball: hitting for average, hitting for power, fielding, throwing, and running. "It doesn't make sense for one person to have all that talent," he said in wonder.

By June 9, Junior had played in fifty-eight games for San Bernardino. He was hitting .338, with 74 hits, including 13 doubles and 11 home runs. He was the number one prospect in the whole California A League and was voted onto the league's All-Star team.

But the game on June 9 was to be the last game he played as a member of the A League. That night, playing center field, he dove after a ball, trying to make an impossible catch. He landed hard and felt a sharp pain in his back. Once again, his fearless play in the field had resulted in an injury.

Junior wound up on the disabled list for two whole months. When he was ready to return, he received some surprising news — he had played so well before his injury that the Mariners were sending him to their AA Eastern League team in Vermont. Once again, Junior had been promoted.

Here, though his back remained sore and he could not play the field yet, he performed well again. As designated hitter, he played in seventeen games, hitting .279, with 2 homers and 10 RBIs. In the Eastern League playoffs, he hit .444!

It had been a great season for Ken Griffey Jr. He had bounced back from the worst crisis of his life. He had been promoted twice and had played like a star wherever they'd sent him. *Baseball America*, for the second year in a row, named him the best major league prospect in the AA Eastern League.

Next year, he figured, he would be promoted to AAA, the last step before the majors. Even with all his confidence and talent, Junior could not have guessed what was really about to happen.

Chapter Five
1989

Making the Team

When Ken Jr. arrived back at home, the whole family was waiting for him. His dad was now back with his original team. Atlanta had traded him to Cincinnati in midseason.

Ken Sr. was almost forty years old — very old for a professional ballplayer — and he hadn't been playing all that well, hitting just .255, his lowest average ever. He knew the Reds might release him at the start of the 1989 season. Still, the elder Griffey hoped he could come back for another year or two of major league ball. In the back of his mind, he harbored a secret dream: that he and his son Kenny would play in the majors together at the same time.

No father and son had ever done it before. Ken Sr. knew it was highly unlikely. After all, he had spent four and a half years in the minors before being promoted. He knew his son was good, but he figured it would take one more year in the minors, at AAA level, before Junior got to the Mariners. Everyone figured that — including the Mariners staff and even Junior himself.

But that was before he arrived at spring training camp. From the very first moment Ken Jr. took to the field, manager Jim LeFebvre and hitting coach Gene Clines knew they were seeing someone special.

Junior had been to his dad's spring training camps ten times growing up. He had been to the Mariners' camp last season, too — so this was actually his twelfth spring training. He felt comfortable with the major leaguers, and he knew he had nothing to lose. Everyone was expecting him to wind up in Calgary, playing for the Mariners' AAA squad. But Kenny knew if he played well enough, there was a chance he'd make the Mariners' major league team.

By the time the exhibition games rolled around, LeFebvre decided to play the nineteen-year-old Griffey in center field every day for the rest of spring training: "Just to get a good look at him," he said.

Junior responded with an incredible exhibition

season. In the field, he made play after magical play: throwing out the speedy Brett Butler with a no-hop strike to third base, making diving catches, and running down balls in deep center. At the plate, Junior was even better. He hit .359 for the exhibition season, including a fifteen-game hitting streak, the longest in Mariner spring training history!

When the time came to cut down the team's roster and send the extra players back to the minor leagues, Ken began to feel nervous. Would he be sent down, too? He had played so well, but there were other, older, more experienced players ahead of him.

Then the call came. The manager wanted to see him. Kenny felt his heart pounding as he entered LeFebvre's office. He expected to hear bad news. But the manager was smiling. "Congratulations," he told Junior. "You're my center fielder."

Kenny felt dizzy with the surprise and realized that he had forgotten to breathe. But he couldn't remember a moment in his life when he'd been so happy.

For LeFebvre and the Mariners staff, the decision had been easy. Young Griffey had surpassed a lot of other people for the center field job, averaging .359, with 32 hits, 49 total bases, and 20 RBIs, and making brilliant plays in center field.

But the Mariners had another reason for promoting Ken Jr. The team was a perennial loser in a small city that had no history of baseball. They needed a star, someone the fans would come to see play. Junior had huge amounts of charisma, energy, and talent — clearly, the moment to introduce him to the Seattle baseball world was now.

Back in Cincinnati, Griffey Sr. also had a good spring, hitting .333 in his first 21 at bats. Now, his improbable dream was about to come true. When the 1989 season began, the Griffeys, Ken Sr. and Ken Jr., became the first father/son team ever to play in the majors at the same time!

Chapter Six

1989–1990

Father and Son

The Mariners' first game of the 1989 season was in Oakland, against the Athletics and star pitcher Dave Stewart. Everyone — the fans, the press, the Mariners' ownership — was waiting to see if Ken Griffey Jr. was as good as his reputation. Would he make it in the major leagues? Or would he fizzle, as so many bright prospects do?

Junior wasted no time in answering those questions. In his very first major league at bat, he smashed a scorching double off the wall in right field!

The next week, the Mariners had their home opener at Seattle's Kingdome, against the Chicago White Sox. Junior came to the plate in the first inning against pitcher Eric King. The whole Kingdome shook with the deafening roar from the crowd, which echoed off the domed stadium's walls and roof.

Then the roar grew even louder as left-hitting Junior took his first swing and launched an enormous home run to the opposite field! The fans gave Junior a rousing standing ovation as he crossed the plate. They had found a new hero — and the Seattle Mariners had gotten themselves a new lease on life.

Junior didn't fade after that first week, either. More than a month later, he was hitting .303, with 3 homers and 9 RBIs. By the All-Star break, his average was .279, his homer total had risen to 13, and he had 38 RBIs. He had stolen 10 bases and played magnificently in center field, making only 3 errors in 81 games!

Yet his name was not on the All-Star ballot that year. Quite frankly, no one had expected him to make it to the majors. Still, almost 80,000 fans added his name to the ballot, making him the number one write-in candidate. It wasn't enough votes to get him onto the All-Star team, but it was close.

Ken Jr. began the second half of the season with high hopes for Rookie of the Year honors. The Mariners had high hopes, too. They had never had a winning year in their entire history. But they were right around .500 now, and with Junior in the lineup, prospects looked bright.

Unfortunately, it was not to be. One cardinal rule of baseball is that the unexpected always seems to happen. On July 25, Junior slipped while getting out of the bathtub in his Chicago hotel room. He landed on his right hand, breaking a bone that ran from his wrist to his pinky. At the time of his injury, several other Mariners were already on the disabled list. Griffey had been hitting .287, with 13 homers and 45 RBIs, but the team had been losing. With Griffey out, the Mariners went into a tailspin.

By the time he came back, on August 20, the Mariners were out of the pennant race. Though he was disappointed, Junior hoped he would be able to help his team win a few more games before the end of the season. He also hoped there was still time for him to catch up with the other Rookie of the Year candidates. He threw himself into each game, trying to make up for lost time with each swing of the bat.

But he was trying too hard, putting too much pressure on himself. For the rest of the season, Griffey hit a mere .181. "I was worrying about hitting the ball seven hundred feet," he admitted later. "I wanted twenty home runs." Manager Jim LeFebvre later commented, "He just lost his poise — which wasn't surprising for a nineteen-year-old kid."

Still, Junior's rookie year numbers were very good: .264 batting average, 16 homers, 61 RBIs, and 23 doubles — in only 127 games! At one point, he tied a Mariner record with 8 straight hits. He had an 11-game hitting streak, was named Player of the Week, and reached base 11 straight times. He excelled in the field as well, with 12 outfield assists, 6 double plays, and dozens of fantastic catches.

His first major league season had been a fantasy come true for Junior, but his sudden fame was not easy to deal with. Fans mobbed him everywhere he went, begging for his autograph. It was suddenly impossible to relax and be himself. Junior was enjoying himself, but all the attention took some getting used to.

He spent hours each week on the phone with his parents. His mom was always available to talk, but it was sometimes hard to reach his dad.

Ken Sr. had been having a good year with the

Reds, hitting .263, with 8 homers and 30 RBIs in 106 games. Even though he was forty years old, he knew he could still play. Junior encouraged his father to keep playing. Who knew? he said. Maybe they'd wind up in the same outfield before Senior retired!

It sounded unlikely. But at the end of the 1989 season, Ken Sr. signed up for another year of baseball. He knew it was Junior's time now, but he still had it in him to keep playing. He didn't take seriously Junior's remarks about their playing together. But the 1990 season held many surprises in store.

Chapter Seven
1990–1991

All in the Family

By the end of 1989, Junior was a nationwide sensation. The fans loved his perfect swing. They loved the long, easy strides he took as he ran down balls in center field. They loved the way the baseball flew out of his hands as he gunned down runners from the warning track. They loved the way he played the game — with intensity, fierce passion, and a kid's broad grin on his face.

That year, Junior became only the second baseball player in history to have a candy bar named after him — the other being the famous right fielder for the Yankees and the A's, Hall of Famer Reggie Jackson.

Still, it had been only one season. Things looked bright for young Ken Griffey, but there were hundreds of stories about baseball phenoms with lots of potential who burned out after one blazing rookie year. When Junior arrived at spring training in 1990, all eyes were once again on the twenty-year-old. Would he continue to improve in his second season?

Ken Griffey Jr., still the youngest player in the major leagues, was ready. He started the exhibition season like a house on fire and stayed hot right on into the regular season. He led the American League in hitting for a while that spring, with an average that reached .395. He was setting the pace with hits, homers, RBIs, and total bases. People looked on in wonder at the kid some were calling "the Natural," after the Robert Redford character in the famous baseball movie.

And Junior, as his amazed coaches were quick to point out, was still a kid. There was no limit to how much better he might get, with a little experience and maturity added into the mix. As his hitting coach, Gene Clines, said, "I don't think anybody's ever been that good at that age."

Junior astounded everyone with the circus catches he kept making in center field. In Oakland, he took a triple away from league-leading hitter Rickey Henderson with an unbelievable catch. The ball was way over his head, but Griffey ran back toward the wall at full speed and, without turning, grabbed the ball over his shoulder.

Then, at the end of April, the Mariners sailed into Yankee Stadium for a big series with the "Bronx Bombers." Young Ken Griffey was about to show the New York fans just how good a fielder he really was.

On the night of April 26, slugger Jesse Barfield came to the plate for the Yankees. He clobbered the ball to left center, the deepest part of the ballpark. Griffey took off after it, his eyes locked on the ball. At the warning track, Junior timed his leap, dug his cleats into the padding of the wall — then ran straight up it!

His glove reached out, well over the top of the eight-foot-high wall, and he snatched the ball. Barfield was already rounding the bases in his home-run trot. Astonished and furious, he glared at Griffey. Junior smiled back, holding the ball up in his mitt for all to see. He had made many great catches in his baseball life, but he knew the home run he had just taken away from Barfield was the best one yet.

The way Griffey played his position inspired the

other Mariners. They had always been a losing team, but now they were diving for balls and making plays as they never had before.

That May, Junior made the cover of *Sports Illustrated* magazine, as "Seattle's 20-Year-Old Wonder." And that's exactly what he was. By mid-July, his batting average was .331, with 40 RBIs, 12 home runs, and 107 hits.

When the All-Star balloting was finished, Ken Griffey Jr. had been voted the starting center fielder — at the ripe old age of twenty. He was the first Mariner ever selected for the All-Star team. It was his first All-Star game, but it would not be his last — not by a long shot.

One month later, his numbers were still high: .323 average, 16 home runs, 56 RBIs. He was second in the league in hitting and was playing the outfield as well as anybody in the game. Ken Griffey Jr. had become a true star. The Mariners had turned around, too — they were over .500 and were growing as a team.

And something else was happening that August: Baseball history was about to be made.

In Cincinnati, Ken Griffey Sr. was still playing

ball, but his career looked like it was almost over. The Reds weren't using him very much. He'd only played in forty-five games and, perhaps because of the lack of playing time — only 68 at bats — he was hitting just .210. The Reds were rebuilding their team, and the forty-year-old was not part of their long-term plans.

On August 18, the Reds announced that they were putting Griffey Sr. on waivers, allowing other teams to claim him. They had first asked him to go on the disabled list to make room for someone younger, but he had refused. He was healthy, he insisted, and was not going to say he wasn't. Now, he was up for grabs. Any team that wanted him could have him.

Seattle owner Jeff Smulyan was quick to see an opportunity. Having father and son play together in the same outfield would bring in thousands of fans. Besides, Griffey Sr. had always been a fine player. Playing with his son might inspire him to play at the top of his game again — not to mention the effect Griffey Sr.'s maturity and leadership in the clubhouse would have on Junior and the other young Seattle players.

So on August 19, the Mariners signed Ken Griffey

Sr. And on August 31, fulfilling Junior's prediction, the Griffeys made history together. They played in the same outfield for the same team — with Junior in center and Senior in left. That night, 27,166 fans, and almost as many people from the press, turned out at the Kingdome to see the magic moment.

How would Senior do under all the pressure? It didn't take long to find out. Kansas City's superstar slugger Bo Jackson was at the plate. He smacked a pitch down the line in left and sped toward first. Jackson was still quite fast in those days, before his hip injury. But Griffey Sr., old as he was, was not exactly slow either. He ran the ball down at the wall, spun around, and fired a bullet to second base. Jackson was out, and the crowd went wild!

Griffey Sr. turned toward his son in center field, and father and son grinned at each other. "It runs in the family," Junior shouted over to him. Later in the game, the two Griffeys singled back to back, doing it at the plate as well as in the field.

For both Griffeys, playing together in the major leagues was the highlight of their baseball lives. In his first week with the Mariners, Griffey Sr. hit .421, with 8 hits and 5 RBIs, in just 19 trips to the plate.

That first week, the Mariners won four of their five games. In September, the Griffeys hit back-to-back home runs against the California Angels. It was another memorable moment.

Senior was playing like a man half his age — like his son, in fact. By the end of the season, he had 3 homers, 18 RBIs, and had hit a whopping .377 for his new team. He had played so well that he decided to come back for one more season in 1991.

As for Junior, he finished the year hitting .300, with a team-leading 80 RBIs and 22 home runs. He had 16 stolen bases, and all his great plays in the outfield had earned him his first Gold Glove, the award given to the best fielder in the league at each position. In just his second season, he had solidified his reputation as a young star of the game.

The Mariners didn't manage to end the season at the .500 mark, though. They finished with 77 wins and 85 losses, in fifth place in the division.

Still, the team was improving. They had a great new pitcher in Randy Johnson, and young Edgar Martinez seemed like a potential batting champion. The future looked bright. Best of all, father and son would be playing together again.

Chapter Eight
1991

All-Star, Gold Glove, Silver Bat

The Griffeys started the 1991 baseball season with great enthusiasm. Everyone was looking forward to seeing them play together in the field on opening day. But it was not to be. During spring training, Ken Griffey Sr. was hurt in a car accident. His neck and back were in pain, and everyone wondered if he would retire.

With Griffey Sr. out, the Mariners started the season badly, losing the first six games they played. Junior saw that the team needed leadership and decided that he was the one to provide it. With his inspired play, the team soon began to do better, and by the third week of the season, Ken Sr. returned.

He did well immediately, and by the end of April, he was hitting .308. Junior was doing even better, hitting .319. And the Mariners had fought their way back almost to the .500 mark, with a record of 12–13.

In May, though, Junior suddenly found himself in a terrible slump. He'd never had a stretch quite so bad. For 18 straight at bats, he went hitless. Still, he didn't let it shake his confidence. Having his dad by his side to encourage him really helped. By the time he finally came out of the slump, with three hits in one game against the Yankees, Junior's average had fallen from .343 to .292. But the Mariners were winning despite Junior's problems, with a record of 23–20.

Then, in mid June, Griffey Sr. went back on the disabled list. His neck had begun bothering him again. Doctors examined him and found a ruptured disk. It meant he would have to sit out at least a month. Would he retire, or would he come back yet again? At midseason, Senior announced that he would try to make it back before the end of the year. His decision cheered Ken Jr. up tremendously.

That July, Junior was a starter on the All-Star team for the second season in a row. He clubbed two singles, and his team, the American League All-Stars, won the game, 4–2. At the All-Star break, the

Mariners were at .500 exactly, with a record of 43–43. Only six and a half games separated them from the first-place Minnesota Twins.

Ken Jr. set his sights on winning the division and caught fire. He hit .410 in July and .377 in August. People were talking about him as a Most Valuable Player candidate, meaning he was more important to his team than perhaps any other player in the league.

The Mariners did not win their division, but they did finish the 1991 season with their first winning record ever, 83–79. And Junior had his best season yet: 100 RBIs, 22 home runs (3 of them grand slams), 42 doubles, 18 stolen bases, and a .327 batting average!

He set team records in batting average, doubles, intentional walks, and slugging percentage. In center field, he made only four errors all season. Once again, he won the Gold Glove — his second straight. This time, he added the Silver Bat award, for the best offensive player at his position. Only Cal Ripken Jr. of the Baltimore Orioles and Griffey won both awards that year. And still Junior was only twenty-one!

Things were not so good for Griffey Sr., though. In September, he needed an operation to repair his torn disk. He was forty-one years old and at that age, he knew coming back from surgery would be tough. So tough, in fact, that he decided to retire as a player. He left the field with a fantastic lifetime average of .296 in nineteen seasons — a great career.

Would his son have an even greater one? Only time would tell. Junior's numbers had improved in each of his three seasons. His batting average had risen from .264 to .300 to .327. He was the first person in the history of baseball to raise his average by 25 points in each of his first three years. But he would have to play many more years before laying claim to a career as impressive as his father's.

Chapter Nine
1992

A New Family

All his life, Ken Griffey Jr. had given his father the credit for much of his success. Besides teaching him right from wrong, his dad had shown him what was really important in life. "Baseball isn't real life," Junior once told reporters. "Family and friends, that's life. . . . My father taught me that, because he never brought it home. Whatever happened at the ballpark stayed at the ballpark."

Ken Sr. had also taught his son how to conduct himself off the field, warning him about the pitfalls of smoking, alcohol, drugs, and other dangerous behaviors. "My parents told me from the beginning," Junior would later say, "I could be a ballplayer or I could be a what-if. I have pride in myself, pride in my family, and pride in my teammates. I wouldn't want to do anything to jeopardize any of those three."

In fact, one of his few missteps as a teenager caught up with him years later. During his rookie season, one of the Seattle newspapers, looking to get its readers' attention, published the story that Junior, as a sixteen-year-old, had been arrested for speeding down a highway at eight-four miles per hour. Ken Jr. could only shake his head, smile, and be thankful that he'd never done anything worse. He knew he had his strong, loving family to thank for that.

Now, in 1992, Ken Griffey Jr. had a new "family": the Seattle Mariners. He had made some good friends on the team: Jay Buhner, a young power-hitting outfielder obtained from the Yankees; Edgar Martinez, the hot-hitting third baseman; and Tino Martinez, the Mariners' new first baseman. These young players, together with pitching ace Randy Johnson, seemed to promise better days ahead for the team.

Just before the start of the 1992 spring training season, Ken Jr. lost a very important member of his biological family. His grandmother Katherine, Alberta Griffey's mother, died of cancer. She and Ken had always had a very close relationship, and her death hit Junior hard. It was the first time in his life that anyone he loved so much had died.

He arrived at spring training with a heavy heart, but didn't tell anyone — not even his friends on the team — what was bothering him. His grief took its toll on Junior's play. He went through a horrendous spring. Some people began to worry about him, but most fans trusted that their hero would come out of it. And sure enough, once the season began, he did.

Soon, he was on his way to another great season. And what made it even greater was that Ken Griffey Jr. was in love.

Her name was Melissa, and Junior had met her three years earlier at a party they'd both gone to because it was alcohol free. Melissa knew Ken was a famous baseball player, but she wasn't much of a fan. In fact, she knew nothing at all about the game. Maybe that was why she was brave enough to ask him to dance.

Now, in 1992, the two decided to get married. The approaching wedding filled Ken with excitement, and he brought that extra enthusiasm to the ballpark every night. He was playing better than he ever had before.

When it came time for the 1992 All-Star game, Ken Griffey Jr. was once again voted onto the starting team. He had played well in his first two All-Star games, but this time, he played even better. He went 3 for 3 at the plate, including a home run off of National League Cy Young Award winner Greg Maddux. Afterward, Junior was voted the game's Most Valuable Player!

Only twelve years earlier, in 1980, he had sat in the stands as his father won the same award. Now, Ken Sr. was the one in the stands, applauding his son's achievement.

By the end of the 1992 season, Junior had put together another fantastic year. He batted .308, the second year in a row he'd gone over .300. He drove in 103 runs, topping 100 RBIs for the second straight time. He hit 27 home runs and collected his third straight Gold Glove award. At age twenty-two, he was a married man and a veteran major leaguer; the sky was the limit for Ken Griffey Jr. And the best was yet to come.

Chapter Ten
1993

Superstardom

After the 1992 season, the Seattle Mariners made some changes, hoping to finally produce a winning team. They fired manager Jim LeFebvre, the man who'd first brought Ken Griffey Jr. to the major leagues. In his place, they hired Lou Piniella. Piniella had been a great player on the 1977–78 championship Yankee teams that featured Reggie Jackson. He had managed the Cincinnati Reds to a world championship in 1990. He was a proven winner — just what the Mariners were looking for.

Piniella then went out and got Norm Charlton, the ace reliever of his Reds championship team, to be Seattle's new closer.

Third, the Mariners signed a new hitting coach — none other than Ken Griffey Sr.!

Junior and Senior met with Piniella as soon as

Leaving a puff of dust below his foot, Ken Griffey Jr. leaps into the air to make an impossible catch.

Ken Griffey Sr. and Ken Griffey Jr. give the press a first look at the only father and son teammates in baseball.

Ken Griffey Jr. and teammate Harold Reynolds proudly show off their 1991 Gold Glove awards.

Though the match against the Minnesota Twins ended his eight-homers-in-eight-games streak, Ken Griffey Jr. is still a champ in the eyes of his father.

AP/Wide World Photos

Ken Griffey Jr. warms up for batting practice; his habit of wearing his hat backward caused an accusation that he didn't respect the game.

Ken Griffey Jr. wears a heavy bandage to help protect his healing fractured wrist.

The Seattle Mariners mob Ken Griffey Jr. after he scores the winning run on a double by Edgar Martinez. The victory gave the team its first chance to play in an American League championship series.

Junior catches a fly ball hit to deep center field.

Safe! Griffey scores on a slide into home, narrowly avoiding the catcher's tag.

With a mighty swing, Griffey slugs a two-run homer.

Ken Griffey Jr.'s Career Highlights

1990–1999
American Leage Gold Glove Award

1990–2000
Member of All-Star Team
(selected in 1995, but unable to play due to injury)

1996–1999
Silver Slugger Award

1991:
American League Silver Bat Award

1992:
Voted Most Valuable Player of the All-Star Game

1993:
Ties league record for hitting home runs in consecutive games (8 games)
Hits 45 home runs
Becomes one of five players to reach 100 RBIs before 24th birthday

1997:
American League Gold Glove Award

1999:
Member of MLB's All-Century Team
Named "Player of the Decade" for the 1990's

Ken Griffey Jr.'s Year-to-Year Major League Statistics

Year	Team	Games	At Bats	Runs	Hits	HRs	RBIs	Avg.	Steals	Put Outs	Fielding Avg.
1989	SEA	127	455	61	120	16	61	.264	16	302	.969
1990	SEA	155	597	91	179	22	80	.300	16	330	.980
1991	SEA	154	548	76	179	22	100	.327	18	360	.997
1992	SEA	142	565	83	174	27	103	.308	10	359	.991
1993	SEA	156	582	113	180	45	109	.309	17	317	.991
1994	SEA	111	433	94	140	40	90	.323	11	225	.983
1995	SEA	72	260	52	67	17	42	.258	4	190	.990
1996	SEA	140	545	125	165	49	140	.303	16	375	.990
1997	SEA	157	608	125	185	56	147	.304	15	388	.985
1998	SEA	161	633	120	180	56	146	.284	20	409	.988
1999	SEA	160	606	123	173	48	134	.285	24	387	.978
2000	CIN	145	520	100	141	40	118	.271	6	375	.987
2001	CIN	111	364	57	104	22	65	.286	2	195	.985
2002	CIN	70	197	17	52	8	23	.264	1	94	.970
Totals		1,861	6,913	1,237	2,039	468	1,358	.292	176	4,306	.985

spring training camp opened. The three men were very excited. They were all convinced that the Seattle Mariners now had a chance of becoming a winning team, maybe even of making the playoffs for the first time in the team's history. In addition to a new manager and a new closer, they had Randy Johnson, perhaps the hardest-throwing pitcher in baseball. They had great home-run power with Jay Buhner and Tino Martinez. They had 1992 batting champion Edgar Martinez. And they had one of the best all-around players in the game: Ken Griffey Jr.

Junior started the year off with a bang and he stayed hot month after month. By the All-Star break, he was near the league lead in almost every category, both offensive and defensive: fifth in outfield assists, second in total bases, third in slugging percentage, third in doubles, sixth in runs scored, fifth in homers, and fifth in hits.

As a team, though, the Mariners ran into problems quickly. Edgar Martinez and Tino Martinez (no relation) went down with injuries that kept them sidelined for most of the season. Without them, the Mariners had to rely on Junior more than ever before.

Fortunately, he was up to the task. Even without

the Martinezes, the Mariners still managed to stay in the pennant race. For the first time, they were not out of the running by mid-July, when the All-Star break came around. They were only playing .500 baseball, but they were in a weak division. The first-place Chicago White Sox were only two games ahead of them.

The Seattle fans had been loyal to a losing team for years, but now, with a chance to win, they flocked to the Kingdome as never before. The Mariners were on their way to breaking the two-million mark for attendance for the first time in their history.

For the fourth straight season, Ken Griffey Jr. was elected to the starting American League All-Star squad. He got more votes than any other player. In fact, people were saying he might be the best player in baseball.

Junior himself disagreed, saying that Barry Bonds, of the San Francisco Giants, had slightly better statistics. Bonds and Junior had been friends for years. Both were sons of famous major leaguers (Barry is the son of Bobby Bonds), and both had tremendous natural talent. But while Bonds was a serious type, Junior was outgoing, friendly, always smiling. He seemed to be having so much fun that fans couldn't help loving him. He reminded them that in spite of all the money some players were making, baseball was still a game meant to be enjoyed.

Barry Bonds wasn't the only one people were comparing Junior to. The early nineties had produced a bumper crop of great young players: Frank Thomas of the Chicago White Sox, Albert Belle of the Cleveland Indians, Juan Gonzalez of the Texas Rangers, and Roberto Alomar of the Toronto Blue Jays were just a few. Some of the older greats were still around, too: Don Mattingly and Wade Boggs of the New York Yankees, Tony Gwynn of the San Diego Padres, and Eddie Murray of the Baltimore Orioles.

Still, Ken Griffey Jr. had become the best loved of all of them. And he was about to add even more luster to his golden image.

On July 20, he hit a home run. It didn't seem remarkable at the time for a young man with so many homers. But when he homered again the next night, and then the next, and the next, and the next, people began to take notice. Junior kept hitting home runs night after night. In the end, he homered in eight straight games — something only two other players (Dale Long of the Pittsburgh Pirates in 1956 and Don Mattingly of the Yankees in 1987) had ever done.

During the fourth game of the streak, Cleveland Indians manager Mike Hargrove decided to try something different to throw Junior off. He had his catcher tell Griffey what pitch was coming. Junior popped out. But the next at bat, the catcher said nothing. And Junior hit it out of the ballpark!

The seventh home run was a grand slam. And the eighth was a 405-foot shot off the Kingdome's third-deck facade. Watching it go, Junior could only smile as the hometown fans roared their approval.

The streak finally ended against pitcher Scott Erickson and the Minnesota Twins. That night, 45,607 fans packed the Kingdome to root for their hero. "If he had hit a home run," Mariners pitcher Erik Hanson said afterward, "the roof would have come off, and we'd have an outdoor stadium."

Junior's remark when the streak finally ended was typical. "I'm not disappointed," he said. "It was fun."

The Mariners finished the 1993 season with only their second winning year ever. Junior led his team in every offensive category. He had a .309 batting average and 45 home runs, led the league in total bases with 359, and made only 3 errors in center field out of 327 chances. Even more impressive, he had 109 RBIs. That meant he had batted in 100 or more runs for three years in a row. There were only four other people in baseball history to drive in 100 or more runs for three straight years before their twenty-fourth birthdays. Their names are Ted Williams, Joe DiMaggio, Mel Ott, and Ty Cobb. All of them are in the Hall of Fame.

Junior also achieved some other milestones during the 1993 season. He became the sixth-youngest player ever to hit 100 homers (at 23 years, 5 months, 25 days). He was the third youngest to hit 20 homers four seasons in a row, the tenth youngest to hit 40 homers in a season, and he had the seventh-greatest number of hits before age twenty-four (832)!

People marveled at Junior's achievements, his grace on the field, and his easy way with fans and the press. They loved his youth and his enthusiasm. Not since Willie Mays, they said, had someone come along with such talent and such charisma. Junior was a superstar at twenty-three — his face had become the face of baseball.

During Ken Griffey Jr.'s first four seasons, the Mariners had the best attendance years in their history. Recognizing Junior's value to their team, the Mariners' new owners offered him a huge four-year contract to stay in Seattle through the 1996 season.

Junior knew he could probably make more money playing in a big city like New York or Los Angeles. But he liked Seattle. He and Melissa had bought a house in a Seattle suburb and were settling in together. He had good friends on the team — Jay Buhner, Edgar Martinez, Tino Martinez, and Randy Johnson. They had all been striving to turn the Mariners around, and Griffey wanted to be with them when they finally came out on top. He signed the contract the Mariners offered him — for four years at $24 million!

Ken Griffey Jr. had now made himself a rich man for the rest of his life. But money was never the reason he played baseball. He played it because he loved the game. He studied statistics night and day, memorized every opposing pitcher's mix of pitches and pick-off moves to first base. He followed the standings and read all the box scores. He was often the first person at the ballpark and the last to leave.

Most of all, he continued to have fun on the ball field. For him, being out on the artificial turf of the Kingdome was just like being a kid on the Cincinnati sandlots. "Baseball is a game to me," he told reporters. "I love to play baseball. I don't think of it as work. I'd play for nothing. And if I couldn't play pro ball, I'd play softball."

Still, big money has a way of changing some people. It was one of the reasons that baseball fans were beginning to stay away from the game. Big stars were starting to refuse to sign autographs or even smile at the fans. But Junior was never like that, and the fans had loved him for it from the very first moment.

Until the end of the 1993 season, Junior had resisted the temptation to make big money off his stardom by doing commercials or endorsements. "I wasn't real comfortable doing commercials or being in the spotlight," he later said, "because I wanted to establish myself on the field first." Well, he'd done that now. And soon he had signed deals with Nike sneakers, Franklin batting gloves, Louisville Slugger bats, Rawlings gloves, Upper Deck baseball cards, and Oakley sunglasses.

When the Nintendo Corporation, new owners of the Mariners, offered to make a video game around him, he accepted. It was called *Ken Griffey Jr. Presents: Major League Baseball*. An avid video-game player himself, Junior was pleased. It was the kind of product he had no trouble endorsing. The company soon had him out promoting the game, playing it with kids from around the country.

That fall, Ken also had a part in his first major motion picture, *Little Big League*. Other major leaguers like Paul O'Neill of the Yankees and Cleveland's Carlos Baerga took part in the project as well. But the hundreds of kids who mobbed the filming location at the Metrodome in Minneapolis, autograph books in hand, were there to see Junior. And he did not disappoint them. At one point, the director asked him to hit a home run into the upper deck, just inside the foul pole in right field. Junior did it perfectly — not once, but three times in a row.

Then the director wanted Ken to make a circus catch in center, leaping over the wall to steal a home run. He asked if he should keep the fans from interfering. Junior told him not to worry. "You see what it says in here?" he asked, holding up his mitt. "It says 'Gold Glove.' Throw the ball up there. I'll catch it." And he did, to the delight of the kids in the stands.

Ken had always loved children and he got along wonderfully with them. So well, in fact, that most people thought of him as a kid himself. But that was about to change. He and his wife, Melissa, were expecting their first child.

Chapter Eleven
1994

The Cap Feud

In January, Ken's wife, Melissa, gave birth to a baby boy. Ken and Melissa didn't want him to go by the name Ken. There were already three of those around (Buddy Griffey's given name was also Ken). Instead they named him Trey Kenneth Griffey — the one and only Trey in the family.

The arrival of his son changed Ken Jr. instantly. He was no longer just himself — he was somebody's daddy now. Just as his own father had sworn to be there for his children, Ken Jr. made himself the same promise. No matter how famous he got, no matter how much the fans and reporters pressed him for his attention, he would always make time and space for his family.

Trey became the apple of his father's eye. The baby had large hands and feet — a future athlete, everyone was soon saying. He also had a wonderful smile, just like his father and grandfather. A true Griffey. "But thank goodness he has his mother's looks," Ken Jr. joked with reporters.

As for being a father, Ken admitted it was a big adjustment. "You think playing ball is hard work?" he asked the press. "Being a father — that's hard work!" He explained that Trey would keep moving around while his father tried to change his diaper. "He picks up one leg, and when I push it down, he picks up the other!"

He admitted to being nervous holding Trey. Even though he had now won four straight Gold Gloves, he still felt shaky carrying such a precious burden.

Obviously, "the kid" was having a wonderful time being "the dad." Being a father showed him what was really important in life. "You could take away baseball," he would later say, "take away all my material things, but I would still have him. That means everything to me."

Soon, though, it was time for spring training again. One person was missing from this year's camp — Ken Sr. had quit his job as the Mariners' hitting coach to become a roving minor league instructor for the organization. Ken Jr. was sad not to have his father around. His dad was still his best coach, spotting everything wrong with his swing or his batting stance.

But Junior understood. His dad was tired of the full-time grind of travel and nightly games. He had been a player for twenty-six years and a coach for two. Senior's new job would allow him time with his wife and daughter at home, and time with Ken Jr.'s brother, Craig, now with the Mariners' Jacksonville minor league franchise. Craig was a good, speedy player, although not a power hitter like his older brother. The Mariners, and Ken Sr., had high hopes that one day soon Craig would make the team, and he and Junior would be teammates.

This year, everyone expected the Mariners to become real contenders for the division championship. They had grown together as a team for a few years now but still had never finished higher than fourth place. Baseball fans in Seattle felt it was time for their team to win.

Unfortunately, as the 1994 season began, the Mariners got off to a poor start. Not Junior, though. The new father was playing inspired baseball now.

His focus and intensity had reached new heights. Ken Griffey Jr. had always been a great all-around ballplayer, but with his 45 home runs during the 1993 season, he had established himself as a genuine power hitter, one of the game's best.

In 1994, Junior started off the season by hitting homers in bunches. He was not the only one — Frank Thomas of the Chicago White Sox, Albert Belle of the Cleveland Indians, and, in the National League, Matt Williams of the San Francisco Giants were all hitting more home runs early on than anyone had in many years.

Soon, fans all over the country were talking about the possibility that someone would break Roger Maris's fabled record of 61 home runs in a single season, set way back in 1961. Since then, no one had seriously challenged the record. But now, major league baseball was expanding, adding new teams. This meant that there were fewer good pitchers to go around. It seemed that everyone was hitting more home runs now. Was 1994 going to be the year Maris's record fell?

There were other exciting things going on in baseball that spring. The National and American leagues had both split into three divisions (from East and West to East, Central, and West), and there was to be a new "wild-card" format for the playoffs. The three division winners and the team with the next-best record would get into post-season play. That meant that more fans from more cities would share in the excitement of pennant races.

But 1994 was also a year of great troubles for major league baseball. The team owners, claiming that many of them were losing money, wanted to make changes in their agreement with the players' union. The players were unhappy with the way the owners were running things and were threatening to go on strike in the middle of the season!

As incredible as the threat seemed, everyone — including the fans — took it seriously. Over the years, baseball had become a business, with a lot of money at stake. Players and owners alike were making more than ever before.

In 1976, the players had won the right to be free agents. That meant they could leave their teams to sign with other teams. They had fought hard to win that right and had even gone on strike a couple of times before to keep it.

So the season began under a dark cloud. As April turned to May, and no agreement came between the players and the owners, fans could only hope that the wonderful season would be allowed to go on to its finish.

By late May, Ken Griffey Jr. was at or near the league lead in home runs, hits, average, slugging percentage, total bases, runs scored, intentional walks, and fielding percentage. But the Mariners were playing poorly.

Ken had always taken winning seriously. It was what he was all about and, until he'd come to the majors, it was what he'd always done. But for four years now, he'd been with a so-so team. He'd been patient, content to watch his teammates grow and improve. But now he became impatient and frustrated. He was ready to win it all — why weren't they?

Near the end of the month, his frustration boiled over, and he complained to the press about his teammates' lack of heart. He later regretted using that expression but insisted he'd meant what he'd said. He even hinted that he might not want to return to Seattle when his contract ran out at the end of the 1996 season. He had proved himself as a player and he was a millionaire several times over. What mattered to him now was winning.

In May, Ken hit his 150th home run. He was the third-youngest player ever to hit that many. Only Hall of Famers Met Ott and Eddie Mathews had done it sooner. With his 153rd homer, he surpassed his dad's career total of 152. In his first 65 games that season, he hit 30 home runs, more than anyone in history except the great Babe Ruth himself. In fact, Junior was on a pace to hit not 60, like Ruth, or 61, like Maris, but 70 home runs for the season!

Naturally, the world was taking notice. Ken had always attracted attention everywhere he went with his play and his charisma. But this was different. In a season of trouble for major league baseball, Junior and the other contenders for the Maris record were keeping the fans excited and happy. Mobs of kids followed him wherever he went. Photographers and reporters dogged his every step. He found that he couldn't go anywhere without being the center of a huge crowd.

His teammates marveled at the way Junior handled all the attention. He was always polite and gracious, signing autographs and shaking hands and answering the same questions day after day after day. Although it was exhausting, he never let it affect his play. Through it all, he kept his sense of humor, too. With his cap on backward in his trademark style, he would mock wrestle with kids and reporters, crack jokes, share a laugh at any time.

He reminded the older reporters of his father, who always used to keep people in stitches with his jokes. Both Griffeys seemed to genuinely enjoy it all. "I played Little League ball for fun," Junior told the press, "and that's the way I play it now."

Still, the crush of publicity was wearing Ken down. He had a wife and a new baby, and all he really wanted to do was be with them — alone. He longed to go fishing or jet-skiing with Melissa, to laugh as Trey sat up for the first time. But even at home, fans constantly surrounded the house. Junior began to sign fewer autographs and sometimes drove straight home after games without signing any. He just needed a little privacy in the midst of all the madness.

Then one day, a threatening letter from a fan arrived in the mail. Apparently, Ken had offended some of his fans by signing too few autographs — and this fan had taken it personally.

Ken was determined to protect his wife and child. He had a high wall built around his estate, got seven guard dogs, and hired four of his childhood friends to act as bodyguards. He hated to do it, but he had to keep himself and his family safe.

In spite of all the pressure and the distractions, Junior's home-run streak continued well into the month of June. Everywhere he went, people were talking about the possibility of his breaking Maris's record. The odd thing was, though he kept up with the records of many current players, until that year, Griffey had barely even heard of Roger Maris! Maris had retired before Junior was even born. And as for Babe Ruth, Junior didn't know much about him, either.

But he was learning fast. He learned that during Maris's legendary season, clumps of his hair fell out from stress. Reporters kept asking Griffey if he, too, was losing hair. He denied it, but told them he was going to grow an Afro just to prove he had enough hair.

On June 21, he hit his 31st home run. No one had

ever hit that many before July 1. The previous record, 30, had been held by Babe Ruth. His 32nd came off pitcher Paul Assenmacher in a series with the Chicago White Sox. It measured over 400 feet. Out of his first 32 homers, 23 had traveled that far.

Before that game, he and fellow home-run record contender Frank Thomas of the White Sox jokingly checked each other's heads for telltale signs of baldness. Then, Junior told Thomas he was going to go deep that night. Thomas said later that he believed him. "I could see it in his eyes," he said.

In spite of his home-run totals, Ken Griffey Jr. had never considered himself primarily a power hitter. He didn't look like one. "They're all six foot four, 225 pounds," he said. "I'm six three, 205. I'm not a big guy. I just try to make contact. I'm the little guy in the group. People always root for the little guy."

The fans sure were rooting for Ken Griffey Jr. That year, they gave him 6,079,688 votes on the All-Star ballot — more votes than any player had ever gotten!

In the weeks before the All-Star game, Ken went into a home-run slump, going eleven games without one. Frank Thomas and Albert Belle closed in on his league lead. But Griffey didn't care. He was focused on one thing only: the Mariners winning.

As always, Ken Griffey Jr. was a team player first and foremost. He played every single game in center field. Even though he was exhausted, he felt his team needed him even more than he needed to rest.

The All-Star game that year was scheduled to take place at Three Rivers Stadium in Pittsburgh, near Griffey's hometown of Donora, Pennsylvania. Ken was excited and planned to invite everyone he knew.

But there's more to the All-Star break than just the game itself. It's a chance for great players who face off against each other all year long to make friends and play as teammates.

When Griffey arrived at the stadium for workouts, his pal Frank Thomas bowed down to him in mock worship. Griffey had to laugh. The two of them were neck and neck in the race to break Maris's record, and Thomas's stats were every bit as good as Griffey's. Still, Thomas understood that Griffey had a charisma that no other star in the game possessed. "He is like a kid on the sandlot," he remarked. "We're all competitors, we all play to win, but he always seems to be having more fun than the rest of us."

Then came the Home Run Derby, in which the game's top sluggers see who can hit the most home runs on a given number of batting practice pitches. Despite all the thick-armed power hitters in the derby, Griffey won the contest with an awesome performance that had the fans going wild.

But the highlight of the All-Star game that year came just before the start of the game itself, when Junior sought out the legendary Reggie Jackson. There on the field, the two of them held a private conversation about fame, pressure, and superstardom. It was as if the king of one baseball era were handing over the torch to the present and future king. There they were — the only two players ever to have candy bars named after them — shaking hands and patting each other on the back. They spoke for a full twenty minutes, with Jackson doing most of the talking.

Later, when reporters asked Jackson what he'd told Griffey, the man nicknamed "Mr. October" for his great World Series performances said: "I told him, 'Make time for your family and friends, find the time to be alone and be yourself. Without that, the burdens will eat you up.' " Good advice from a man who knew. As for Junior, Jackson had this to say: "He's everything we would like to be. He's young, he's good looking, he's got the best smile in the world, and he's a heroic athlete. He is what this game needs right now."

In fact, Junior had become what many other baseball stars were not — a role model. He was friendly, polite, a good sport, a great athlete, and he had never gotten involved in drugs, alcohol, or other dangerous behaviors.

Which is why it was surprising to everyone when in late July, Yankee manager Buck Showalter said in a radio interview that he disliked Griffey's wearing his cap backward. Showalter claimed that Griffey was showing a lack of respect for the game of baseball. "A guy like Ken Griffey Jr., the game's boring to him. He comes on the field and his shirttail is hanging out. . . . " Those were Showalter's words.

When Griffey heard about this, he was talking to reporters in the clubhouse. His cap was on backward, as it usually was before or after the game (but never during). Junior was shocked to hear what Showalter had said about him. "He doesn't know me," he said, "and I don't know him. I said hi to him once. I haven't sat down and eaten lunch with him." As to wearing his cap backward during workouts, he said, "I'm not going to change for one person. I've had my hat on this way since I was a kid. I'm not going to change now."

It was a diplomatic response — Junior was careful not to say anything negative about Showalter in return. His manager, his teammates, and fans all across the country stuck up for him in what became known as the "cap feud." "If you watched this kid play every day, he plays as hard as anyone in the league," said Mariners manager Lou Piniella. "And he plays every day."

In early August, the Eastern Division–leading Yankees came to Seattle to play the Mariners (who were in last place in the Western Division, in spite of Junior's league-leading home-run pace). When Showalter and his team came on the field, they were startled to see all the Mariners, even ex-Yankee Goose Gossage, wearing their caps backward! "It's a show of solidarity," Mariners third baseman Mike Blowers told the press.

But the cap feud wasn't the only thing distracting

reporters from the race to break Roger Maris's home-run record. Since the beginning of the season, the players had been threatening to go on strike and bring the season to a screeching halt. Now, every baseball fan's worst nightmare was about to come true.

Chapter Twelve
August 1994–April 1995

The Strike

On August 11, 1994, Ken Griffey Jr. hit his 40th home run of the season — a grand slam. But it was to be his last that year. The next day, the baseball strike began. At the time of the strike, Junior stood 2 homers ahead of Frank Thomas (38) and 4 ahead of Albert Belle (36) for the American League lead. In the National League, San Francisco's Matt Williams led the majors with an incredible 43 home runs!

When the strike began, no one knew how long it would last. Some said days; some said weeks. No one imagined that it would last the rest of the season, the whole winter long, and into the beginning of the 1995 season. Yet that is exactly what happened. Both sides — the players and the owners — held hard and fast to their bargaining positions. The players lost their salaries, and the owners lost their profits, but the biggest losers were the fans. They lost baseball — their favorite pastime. Roger Maris's home-run record survived its stiffest challenge, not because any of the players fell short, but because the season ended too soon.

Ken Griffey Jr. had every reason to be against the strike. He stood to lose more than most baseball players — namely, the chance to go down in history as the man who broke Maris's record. But he expressed no bitterness about it. Instead, he came out firmly, if sadly, in favor of the strike. "My dad lived through a strike, and so will I," he said. "The union did what was best for the players." He knew that the baseball strikes of the past had helped the players get their fair share of the profits.

As for what he planned to do if the strike became a long one, he answered, "I'll just play my second career. Vacationing." For Junior, that meant spending lots of time at home with Melissa, Trey, his parents, brother, sister, and friends. It meant fishing, video games, and quiet times.

But it also meant lots more commercial endorsements and lots of charity work. Ever since Junior had come up to the big leagues, he'd been sought after to help many worthy causes. And he never said no, as long as time permitted. The first time he'd done charity work was in 1990, for the Make-A-Wish Foundation. The foundation grants wishes for seriously ill children, many of whom want to meet superstars like Ken Griffey Jr.

So in 1990, Junior found himself taking a young boy with cancer to dinner. The boy fell asleep in the limousine on the way home, with his head on Junior's shoulder. That did it for Ken. From then on, he did all the charity work he could. "Imagine how Griffey feels when a kid can have anything, meet anyone in the world he or she wants, and they choose to meet him. That's a lot of pressure." So said the marketing director of the Seattle chapter of Make-A-Wish. "Ken has been wonderful. He has never, ever turned us down."

The fall of 1994 came and went, with no World Series. It was the first time since the series originated in 1904 that it had failed to take place.

The absence of baseball left a huge void in the hearts of millions of Americans. They became angry, blaming both the players and the team owners for taking their game away from them. Many vowed that they would never again return to the ballpark or watch a baseball game on TV. Instead, they swore, they would turn to football, or hockey, or basketball — even minor league baseball.

The winter of 1994–95 passed, and there was still no agreement to play. No one knew if there would be baseball in 1995. The owners were now threatening to fire all the players and bring in replacements. Everyone knew this would not be real major league baseball. But the owners hoped to pressure the players into reaching an agreement.

Things went from bad to worse. When spring training time rolled around and nothing had been settled, Ken Griffey Jr. started to get impatient. He had been robbed of a chance to break the home-run record. He had finished the shortened season with astounding numbers: 40 homers and 90 RBIs in only 111 games, with a .323 batting average and a fifth Gold Glove. But he wanted more. He wanted to be a part of a winning team, and he wondered if and when he would ever get the chance.

Finally, at the beginning of April, just as the owners were about to open the regular season with replacement players, the word went out: The long strike had been settled! There would be a short spring training, followed by a slightly shortened season.

Baseball was back!

The only question now was: Would the fans return?

The fans quickly gave their answer. Attendance for the early season games was way down all across the country. Only in Boston's Fenway Park, where the Red Sox jumped out to a huge early season lead in the American League East, did the fans return full force.

In Seattle, there were thousands and thousands of empty seats. Many people felt that one reason the fans were staying away was because they didn't like coming to the Kingdome. The Kingdome had always been an unpopular stadium. It had plastic turf and a gray concrete roof. It had been compared to a big airplane hangar, and once even to a tomb. The year before, falling roof tiles had forced the Mariners to close the stadium and play several of their home games in other places. During the repairs, which cost $51 million, a worker had been killed. The Kingdome was considered the very worst stadium in all of baseball.

The owners of the Mariners had told the city that unless a new stadium was built, the team would leave Seattle forever when their lease was up. The team's owners had already drawn up the plans for a gorgeous new facility, with real grass, a retractable roof, and views of the Seattle skyline, the harbor, and Mount Rainier. It would, they claimed, draw thousands more fans and help the team, which had lost $20 million the year before, be profitable again. It would be known, they said, as "the house that Griffey built."

But a new stadium costs millions of dollars. This one, they said, would cost $270 million. The team's owners were willing to pay $45 million of it themselves. But that left $225 million to be raised. Where was that money going to come from?

The mayor and city council decided that they would have to get the money from the people of Seattle by raising their taxes. To do that, they would have to put the matter to a vote. They scheduled the vote for late September.

Would the people of Seattle vote to pay for a new

stadium? It didn't seem likely — especially in the aftermath of the strike. The thought of abandoning Seattle and moving to another city made Ken Griffey Jr. sad. He loved his adopted home and he didn't want the Mariners to leave.

To Junior, the key to getting the fans back, the key to getting the people of the city to vote for a new stadium, was to give them a winning team. He cared so much about making the Mariners winners that two years before, he and two other players had volunteered to delay getting part of their salaries so that the team would have enough money to bring in more good ballplayers. The players' union didn't allow the deal to go through, but it showed how much Junior cared about playing for a winning team.

Ken knew that this had to be the year Seattle produced a winner. And as usual, he felt that it was up to him to lead his team to victory.

Chapter Thirteen
1995

A Season of Destiny

During the short spring training season, everyone in the Mariners camp had high hopes for a winning season. They were all excited to be back playing ball again.

Junior was in such a good mood that he let loose with a rash of practical jokes. No one, not even the coaching staff, was safe. One day, during batting practice, Lou Piniella bet Ken a steak dinner that he couldn't hit a certain pitch. Griffey swung at it and missed. Instead of taking his manager to a restaurant for his steak, Junior did something better. The next week, when Piniella got to his office in the clubhouse, he found a 1,200-pound cow standing there! "There's your steak dinner," said Junior with a smile.

When the season finally started, the Mariners got

off to the best start in their history. By May 26, they had a record of 14–12 and were only a few games out of first place. But attendance continued to lag.

That night, they played a home game against the Baltimore Orioles. Early in the game, Junior hit his seventh home run of the young season. By the seventh inning, the Mariners were ahead, 4–3, when Kevin Bass came to the plate for the Orioles.

Bass swung for the fences, trying to hit a game-tying home run. He launched the ball deep into center field, way over the head of Griffey, who always played shallow. Junior ran after it full speed, out to the warning track, out to the wall. His eyes were on the ball. He knew the wall was there, but he couldn't slow down or he'd have no chance to make the catch.

He leaped a full four feet into the air at a dead run, putting out his left hand to brace himself as he crashed into the wall. Incredibly, he came down with the ball in his glove! But his left wrist had taken the brunt of the impact with the wall. Griffey fell to the turf, wincing in pain.

The crowd at the Kingdome had cheered wildly when Griffey caught the ball. Now they held their collective breath as their hero lay writhing in agony. The trainers ran out to tend to him, then brought Griffey into the clubhouse as the crowd gave him a standing ovation. Everyone knew that Junior was hurt. The only question was how seriously.

The answer came later that night, and the news was bad: Junior had fractured his wrist, breaking the bone in seven places. The next morning, he had two hours of surgery. Doctors attached a two-inch-long metal plate to his wrist with seven screws to hold the bone in place while it healed. They told reporters it would be three months before Griffey could play again.

It was the most serious injury Ken Griffey Jr. had ever had. He had always played the field recklessly, not worrying about getting injured. Now he was paying the price.

He had made the catch — a catch Orioles manager Phil Regan called the best he'd ever seen. The Mariners had won the game. But now they would have to play without their leader through the rest of May, June, July, and August. Could they stay close enough to first place to catch up in September, when Junior returned?

Mariners fans were devastated. Their hopes of winning the vote, building a new stadium, and keeping the team in Seattle seemed to have vanished in one horrible instant.

Junior, too, was upset. But he was determined to get back as quickly as he could. In the meantime, he promised to be in the dugout with his teammates, cheering them on.

Griffey's dedication to the team seemed to inspire his teammates. They went on to win four of their next five games, giving them a league-best 12–4 record at home. Three of the victories came in a sweep of Buck Showalter's Yankees.

During one of the games of that series, Mariners ace pitcher Randy Johnson hit Yankee catcher Jim Leyritz in the face with a 96-mile-per-hour fastball. Leyritz fell to the ground and lay there for several minutes. When he finally managed to get up, he shouted at Johnson, threatening to hurt him if he ever saw him outside the stadium.

The incident escalated the bad feelings between the two teams. The fight over Junior's cap had started it, and this just made things worse. Yankee captain Don Mattingly, a great player who had never been to the playoffs in his long, illustrious career, said of the pitch, "There's absolutely no doubt in my mind that that was intentional. If he can't hit a batter without hitting him in the head, he shouldn't be doing it at all."

Showalter got so angry at Johnson that the umpires ejected the Yankee manager from the game.

Johnson denied afterward that he'd hit Leyritz intentionally, but the Yankees clearly didn't believe him. They swore to get even by beating Seattle the next time the two teams met.

The Mariners continued to play good ball without Griffey, but another team was ahead of them in their division. The California Angels were on fire. By the All-Star break, the Angels were way ahead of the other three teams in the Western Division. Everyone was convinced they would win the West, with Boston winning the East, and the awesome Cleveland Indians taking the Central Division. That left only the new wild-card playoff spot up for grabs.

The Mariners were still in the thick of the fight. If they could stay close for just one more month, they'd have Junior back, and a legitimate chance to earn the fourth spot and make the playoffs for the first time in their sixteen-year history.

Even though he'd only played one month's worth of baseball that season and had sat out ever since with a broken wrist, Ken Griffey Jr. was still a favorite of the fans. They marked in his name on the All-Star ballot even knowing he wouldn't be able to play in the game. He registered 1,204,748 votes and made the starting team for the sixth straight time!

Ken rented a private jet to fly to the All-Star game. "The fans took the time to punch my name out on the ballot even though they knew I couldn't play," he said. "It was important for me to show my appreciation."

Yes, the fans loved Junior. But without him, would Seattle fans continue to come to the Kingdome? As July turned to August, and the California Angels widened their lead over the Mariners to thirteen and a half games, attendance began to plummet. If the fans weren't coming, would the Seattle voters approve the new stadium? And if they didn't, would major league baseball leave Seattle forever?

Chapter Fourteen
August–October 1995

Refuse to Lose!

When Junior returned to the Mariners lineup on August 14, things looked bleak. The Mariners had gone 43–42 without him, which was better than everyone had expected. Still, most people felt that the Western Division race was over, with California the sure winner. The Mariners, twelve and a half games behind the Angels, were struggling to stay in the wild-card race. The competition was fierce: the Texas Rangers, the Kansas City Royals, the Milwaukee Brewers, the Baltimore Orioles, the Oakland A's, and the New York Yankees were all in good position.

In only his second game back, with the Mariners visiting the Minnesota Twins, Griffey singled in the first inning. It was the 1,000th hit of his career. At twenty-five years old, he was the seventh-youngest player ever to get there. Their new left fielder, Vince Coleman, started a five-run rally in the eighth, and the Mariners came from behind to win, 6–4.

The Mariners returned home in mid-August to face the struggling Yankees. The Yanks had fallen out of the race for first place in the East, so they, too, needed the wild card to get into the playoffs.

In the first game, the score was tied in the ninth when Junior came to bat. In a moment that was to shape the rest of the Mariners' magical season, he belted a two-run homer off Yankee closer John Wetteland to win the game. Junior raised his arms in triumph as the ball sailed into the right field stands. It was the first time in his career he had ever hit a game-winning home run. Unfortunately, only 17,000 fans were there to see it.

The Mariners went on to win the next two games — one a shutout victory by Randy Johnson — before losing the last game of the series to the Yanks.

When the Bronx Bombers left Seattle, no one in the stands would have guessed they would be back for an epic playoff battle five weeks later. The Yankees looked like a beaten team, and the Mariners were in trouble, too. Randy Johnson went down with stiffness in his back and shoulders. Junior was struggling at the plate, trying to get back into form after his injury. And the fans were getting restless. The vote on the stadium was scheduled for September 19.

Junior was edgy. He snapped at reporters when they asked him about the empty seats in the stadium, saying he and his teammates were trying to bring a winner to the city and needed the fans' support. He hadn't given up on winning the Western Division, either — unlike most people. "We still got a month of baseball," he insisted. "Anything can happen. California could fall apart."

Those last words turned out to be prophetic. The Angels were about to go into one of the all-time worst nosedives in baseball history.

By the time the Mariners got to Yankee Stadium on September 5, a lot had changed. Seattle was leading the wild-card race and they had closed to within five and a half games of the Angels, losers of fifteen out of their last eighteen games! The Yankees were doing better, too. They had gotten back to .500 — but they were still a long way back in the race for the wild card.

Without Randy Johnson available to pitch, the

Mariners lost the first game of the three-game set, 13–3, as the Yankees beat up on a trio of rookie Mariners pitchers — Salomon Torres, Jim Mecir, and Scott Davison. They came back dramatically to win the second game, going ahead 6–0 on solid hitting, including a Griffey homer. They then held on by the skin of their teeth to win, 6–5. But in the finale of the series, the Yanks came from three runs behind to win, 4–3, behind the gutsy pitching of their ace, Jack McDowell.

The last two games were classics, with great play from both teams. "I think it's going to come down to us and them," McDowell said after the final game, boldly predicting that the Yankees would grab the wild card and that the Mariners would overtake the Angels to win the West.

On September 19, the day of the big Seattle stadium vote, Griffey hit a home run against the Texas Rangers to bring his team back from a 4–1 deficit. Then he drove in the game-winning run in the eleventh inning. The win put the Mariners only a game behind the Angels. They dared not look back — one game behind the Mariners stalked the resurgent Yankees.

Thanks to the great late-season comeback by the Mariners, the stadium vote was as close as the league standings — so close that the final results wouldn't be known until the write-in votes were counted.

Playing wild-card rival Texas again the next night, Griffey made a sensational catch in center field to rob slugger Juan Gonzalez of an extra base hit. Junior also homered in the game. He was now back in top hitting form — and not a moment too soon. The Angels lost again that night. The Mariners were now tied for the lead in the Western Division!

On September 21, a crowd of 51,500 showed up at the Kingdome. That night, Seattle rallied from six runs down to beat the Oakland A's. Griffey homered yet again — his third in three games and the fifteenth of his short season. So did Edgar Martinez, who was closing in on another American League batting championship. Newly acquired Vince Coleman added a grand slam to complete the incredible victory.

That night, the Angels lost yet again. Seattle was now in first place in the Western Division! It was the first time they'd ever led their division past May in their entire history.

Only the news that the stadium measure had failed by just a few votes dimmed the spirits of the team and its fans. But that feeling passed quickly. The people of Seattle had gone baseball crazy. The Mariners went on to sweep Oakland. Seattle drew a total of 152,803 fans for the three-game series. While the city government scrambled to find another way to pay for a new stadium, the fans rallied to their beloved team. The slogan "Refuse to Lose!" became the battle cry heard all around the city.

On September 26, the Angels came into the Kingdome for two games — the final games the Western Division rivals would play that season. Junior and Jay Buhner both homered that night, and Seattle won, 10–2. Since Griffey's return, the team had won a scorching 22 of 30 games. During the same stretch, the Angels had gone 9–27.

The Angels won the next game to keep their season alive. But the Mariners picked up the pieces and kept on winning. On September 28, they beat the Texas Rangers, 6–2, with an eighth-inning grand slam from Junior. The loss eliminated Texas from the wild-card race. Randy Johnson got the win to go 17–2 for the season.

With only two games left in the season, and the Boston Red Sox having clinched the Eastern Division and the Cleveland Indians the Central, three teams were still in contention for the remaining two playoff spots — the Yankees, the Angels, and the Mariners. On September 29, the Mariners clinched a tie with the California Angels for the Western Division title with a 4–3 victory over the Rangers in Texas. But the Angels beat the A's that night to stay alive — one game back with one to go.

It was a nerve-racking finish to the season. For six years, Junior had dreamed of going to the playoffs with his Mariners. Now he stood on the verge of achieving that dream. But nothing was final. It was possible that the Mariners would win neither the West nor the wild card. The race was that close.

And indeed, the next day brought no relief. The Mariners lost to the Rangers, while California beat Oakland. That meant that the Mariners and the Angels had ended the season tied for the Western Division lead! A one-game winner-take-all tie-breaker was scheduled for the next day.

The winner would go to the playoffs. The loser

would go home — the Yankees, with a win in their final game, had clinched the wild card. The whole city of Seattle held its breath as the Angels invaded the Kingdome to face Seattle's ace, Randy Johnson.

Johnson was pitching on three days' rest — one day less than normal. But if he was tired, he didn't show it. He retired the first seventeen Angels he faced, struck out twelve, and took a shutout into the ninth inning. The Mariners won their first division championship, 9–1!

It had been an incredible six weeks. The team had been thirteen and a half games out of first place in mid-August, but with Junior back, and the addition of Vince Coleman in left field, Norm Charlton as the closer, and Andy Benes as starting pitcher, the Mariners had achieved the third-greatest comeback in baseball history. Since the night when Junior had homered off John Wetteland in the Kingdome, the Mariners had gone on to win 25 of their last 35 games.

There was no rest for the champagne-soaked players, however. Right after their short celebration, they had to board a plane for the late flight to New York. The playoffs were to begin the very next night!

Chapter Fifteen
October 1995

The Playoffs

"No sleeping on the plane!" Junior Griffey jokingly told his teammates on the way to New York for the first two games of the American League playoffs. The Yankees were going to be a tough team to beat. They had their captain, Don Mattingly, or "Donnie Baseball," as he was known in New York, back from injury and thirsting for his very first playoff victory. They had a new pitching ace, David Cone, to go with Jack McDowell.

For their part, the Mariners would not be able to pitch Randy Johnson again until Game Three back in Seattle. Even then, he'd be pitching on short rest for the second time in a row. Could he keep it up?

It had been a great September, and October promised to be even better for the Mariners. They had drawn an incredible half million people to the

Kingdome for their last ten home games. At last, the whole city of Seattle seemed in favor of the new stadium. They loved their Mariners. Atop the famed Space Needle downtown, a lit-up sign read "Refuse to Lose!"

Ken Griffey Jr. had waited all his life for this moment. With Randy Johnson tired and out of action for two games, the load would fall on the offense — and that meant Junior. His wrist was only about 90 percent better, but it would have to be enough. He was ready.

The media pressure was even more intense now than it had been during the Seattle late-season comeback. But Junior was not shaken by all the attention. It had been coming his way ever since he'd made the team as a nineteen-year-old. He focused on one thing: winning.

In spite of all the excitement, Ken did manage to get an hour or so of sleep on the plane. When he arrived at his hotel room at three-thirty a.m., he had to watch part of a pay-per-view movie he'd already seen just so he could calm down enough to fall asleep. Then he slept like a baby. "Sleep is one of my strong points," he joked with reporters the next morning. "Getting out of bed is more my problem."

He felt better after the few hours' sleep. He couldn't wait to get to the ballpark. He arrived at Yankee Stadium early, his head full of memories. Here, as a young teenager, he'd played pickoff with the sons of Lou Piniella, Don Baylor, Bobby Meacham, and Tom Trebelhorn while the fathers practiced. Billy Martin, the Yankees' scrappy manager, had yelled at them whenever they got too wild, and even kicked them out once or twice.

In many ways, Ken Griffey Jr.'s young career had already surpassed that of his father. He had more home runs, had made more money, and was far more famous. But his father had three world championship rings. Junior had none.

"This is what it's all about," Ken Sr. had said to his young children, showing them the rings. "No matter what people say about you, they can't take that away from you, that you won something that not a whole lot of people win."

Junior walked the familiar clubhouse hallways surrounded by the ghosts of playoffs past: Babe Ruth, Lou Gehrig, Joe DiMaggio, Mickey Mantle,

Yogi Berra, Roger Maris, Reggie Jackson . . . Of all the places to start a playoff, Yankee Stadium was the one place everybody wanted to be.

Ken Sr. would be in the stands that night, along with the whole family. Melissa was expecting their second child. This was Junior's moment, and he intended to seize it.

Before the game, Reggie Jackson paid a visit to the Mariner clubhouse — to say hello to his old friend and teammate Lou Piniella, and to speak with Griffey. Afterward, when reporters asked him if he'd like to inherit Jackson's nickname, Mr. October, Junior answered that he was going to rub his bat against Jackson for good luck.

Feeling confident and determined, Junior stepped onto the field. Yankee Stadium was packed with 57,126 screaming fans. "It was the most amazing crowd I've ever seen," Yankee pitcher David Cone later said. Buck Showalter ran onto the field pumping his fist in the air. When Don Mattingly was introduced, the crowd went berserk.

Showalter had told all his pitchers to pitch carefully to Griffey. Junior had a career .362 average in Yankee Stadium, with 7 homers and 62 RBIs. But

David Cone wasn't careful enough. In the fourth inning, Cone threw a forkball, and Griffey hit a monstrous shot off the facade of the upper deck in right field. It was the first playoff run scored in the history of the Seattle franchise, and it quieted the New York crowd, at least for the moment.

The Yankees had taken an early lead on a two-run homer by Yankee superstar Wade Boggs. Griffey's home run brought Seattle back into the game. But the Yankees had been playing inspired baseball for weeks and they weren't about to stop now. They came back with a two-out rally in the fifth, and soon led the game again, 4–2.

David Cone had been pitching tough, keeping the Mariners in check — except for Griffey. When Junior came to the plate in the seventh with a man on base, Cone resolved not to pitch him another forkball. Instead, he threw him a change-up. Griffey rocketed it into the right field seats for a two-run homer — his second of the game!

With the score now 4–4, Don Mattingly told his teammates in the dugout, "We got a game again, so let's go!" They did. In their half of the inning, Ruben Sierra hit a two-run homer to key a four-run rally.

The Mariners never recovered, losing the game, 9–6. Of all the Mariners, only Griffey had had success against David Cone, going three for five with the two home runs. It had been a great battle, but it was just the beginning of a playoff series that would go down in history as one of the greatest and most exciting ever.

Game Two featured another frenzied Yankee Stadium sellout crowd of 57,126. Andy Pettitte, the Yankees' star rookie, took the mound against the Mariners' recent free-agent pickup Andy Benes. The game seemed to be crucial for both teams. If the Mariners lost, they would have to win all three games in the Kingdome to beat the Yankees in this short best-of-five series. On the other hand, if they could split the two games in New York, the Yankees would have to win two on the Mariners' home turf.

The Mariners took an early 1–0 lead on a Vince Coleman homer, but the Yankees came right back to tie the score. Again, Seattle went ahead, 2–1. Then, in the bottom of the sixth, Yankee designated hitter Ruben Sierra smashed a home run into the right–center field bleachers to tie the score at 2–2. The crowd went wild. The fans had been unruly the

109

night before, and now they threatened to erupt again.

The next man up to the plate was Mattingly, the leader and inspiration of his team. He tore into a 1–0 pitch and hit it to the same spot as Sierra's drive — the first playoff home run of his career — giving the Yankees their first lead of the game, 3–2.

The celebration was thunderous. Fans began raining debris onto the field. Cups and bottles, grapefruit, caps, and helmets littered the whole place. Fearing for his players' safety, Piniella called the Mariners off the field until order was finally restored and the debris carted off.

It was a canny move by Piniella. He wanted to stop the Yankees' momentum, and the fans had given him an excuse to do it. When the game resumed, the Yankee rally ended. The Mariners went ahead in the next inning, 4–3. But the Yanks came back with a Paul O'Neill home run off reliever Norm Charlton, tying the score at 4–4.

That's how it remained until the twelfth inning, when Ken Griffey Jr. stepped up to the plate. He was facing none other than Yankee closer John Wetteland, the man he'd homered off to win the game in August that had started the Mariners on their playoff run.

Wetteland was pitching in his fourth inning, much longer than he usually went. Junior made him pay, rocketing a 3–1 fastball over the wall in right-center. Home run! The Mariners rejoiced. The marathon game, with its clutch hitting and fantastic fielding, looked to be almost over.

But in the bottom of the twelfth, the Yankees came back yet again. Ruben Sierra came to the plate with two men on base. He crushed a pitch from Tim Belcher to left field. Wade Boggs scored easily from second base, and it looked as if Bernie Williams would come across with the winning run all the way from first base. But a perfect throw from Alex Diaz and a perfect relay to catcher Dan Wilson nailed Williams at the plate. The marathon game continued.

The game became a pitchers' duel again, with Belcher now going against Yankee rookie Mariano Rivera. Then, in the bottom of the fifteenth, Jim Leyritz came up to bat — the same Jim Leyritz who had sworn revenge after being hit in the head by Randy Johnson. True to his words, Leyritz hit a two-run homer off Belcher to win the game.

The Yankees mobbed their teammate while the Mariners stared at the celebration in disbelief. After over five hours, 470 pitches, 6 home runs, and enough excitement for a month of baseball games, they had lost. They flew home two-time losers, facing possible elimination and the end of their magnificent season.

Chapter Sixteen
October 1995

From the Jaws of Defeat

But the Mariners were not done yet. They were about to live up to their slogan: "Refuse to Lose!"

In Game Three, Randy Johnson took over. Coming to the mound with only three days' rest for the second time in a row, Johnson pitched one of the grittiest games of his career. He struck out ten and allowed just two runs and four hits in seven innings. The Mariners won their first postseason game in franchise history, 7–4. They now trailed the series 2–1, with two games to go.

Game Four was another one for the history books. New York, behind Scott Kamieniecki, got off to a 5–0 lead before the Mariners staged an improbable comeback to win, 11–8. Ken Griffey Jr. homered again — off Sterling Hitchcock in the fifth — to give Seattle its first lead of the game, 6–5. That made four homers in four games for Griffey. He was indeed following in Reggie Jackson's footsteps and turning into the new Mr. October.

But the hero of Game Four was batting champ Edgar Martinez. With a grand slam to break the game open and a three-run shot before that, Martinez tallied seven RBIs to power the Mariners into the fifth and deciding game of the series.

The fans at the Kingdome shook the building with their stomping and roaring. "It seems like going to the last game is the way it should be," commented Don Mattingly. "It'll be exciting."

Game Five promised to be the greatest contest yet between the two rival teams, and it did not disappoint. Yankee ace David Cone was on the mound again, and he held the Mariners scoreless until the third inning. Then they broke through on a Joey Cora home run. But Paul O'Neill hit a two-run shot in the third to give the Yanks the lead, 2–1. In the fourth, Jay Buhner drove in the tying run. The score was 2–2.

Then, in the sixth inning, Don Mattingly drove in two runs for the Yankees. Things did not look good for Griffey and the Mariners. But the game wasn't over yet.

Ken Griffey Jr. stepped up to the plate against Cone in the bottom of the eighth. With one sweet, perfect swing of his patented thirty-one-ounce bat, he hit his fifth home run of the series! It brought the Mariners to within one, and by the time the inning was over, they had tied the game against a tiring David Cone, who left the game.

With the Yankees threatening in the top of the ninth, Lou Piniella took pitcher Norm Charlton out of the game and inserted none other than Randy Johnson. Johnson, exhausted from so much pitching in the past week, managed to get the Mariners out of the jam and hold the Yankees scoreless until the eleventh.

In that inning, New York finally broke through for a run against Johnson. But Lou Piniella did not take his ace out of the game. A tired Randy Johnson, he felt, was still better than anyone else. Johnson went on to strike out Jim Leyritz and Bernie Williams.

The Mariners had one last chance at bat. They were trailing 5–4. The new Yankee pitcher was their ace, Jack McDowell, back on short rest because John Wetteland had been overused and hit hard by the Seattle sluggers. But McDowell could not hold the Mariners either. It seemed that no one could stop this team. Joey Cora led off with a bunt single. Griffey then singled to center, and Cora went to third.

Up came Edgar Martinez. The entire crowd of over 57,000 was standing and screaming for a hit. And Martinez gave them what they wanted. He smashed a double to left field. Cora scored, tying the game. Could Griffey make it home, all the way from first base?

From the moment the ball was hit, Junior was off and running at full speed. He never stopped coming. He beat the throw home! While he was mobbed by his teammates, the Kingdome exploded in fireworks and deafening noise. The Mariners had won!

They had come from behind, two games to none, to outplay the Yankees in three straight games — and not just any games, but epic, seesaw playoff battles! They had won the first division championship in team history. Junior Griffey's dream had come true!

The series was one for the ages. It was the first playoff ever decided in the final game, in extra innings. Manager Lou Piniella called it "a phenomenal series. It's a shame there has to be a loser, because it was so well played and so competitive."

The Yankees went home devastated. And the Mariners looked ahead two days to their next challenge: the American League championship series, against the awesome Cleveland Indians.

The series with the Yankees had drained every ounce of energy from the Mariners. Randy Johnson and all the other pitchers were spent. Seattle would have to pitch a rookie in Game One. Could they keep their Cinderella season going?

The Mariners actually managed to win Game One, 3–2, behind rookie pitcher Bob Wolcott. But the exhaustion, jet lag, and constant pressure then began to take their toll.

In Game Two, Junior hit a home run in the sixth inning off Orel Hershiser. It was his sixth of the playoffs — tying a major league record. But the homer would be his last of the playoffs. The Indians won the game, 5–2, to earn a split and send the series back to Cleveland for the next three games.

Game Three provided more Seattle heroics, this time in the person of Jay Buhner. After Cleveland had walked Junior intentionally, Buhner won the game with his second homer of the night, a three-run shot in the eleventh inning. Randy Johnson went eight innings for the Mariners, keeping them in the game, giving up only one run. Seattle was alive and well, and the series would now go back to the Kingdome.

But the Indians won the next two games, taking the momentum away from the exhausted Mariners. Cleveland shut Seattle down, 7–0, in Game Four.

Ironically, that same night, Washington's state senate passed a bill approving and paying for a new stadium in Seattle. It was now official — the Mariners had won over the people of the city with their courageous play and refusal to accept defeat. They were staying in Seattle!

Game Five proved to be the turning point of the series. With the Mariners leading 2–1 in the sixth inning, Cleveland third baseman Jim Thome hit a two-run homer to give the Indians a 3–2 lead. Orel Hershiser, who has yet to lose a postseason game in his long career, shut down the Mariners with able relief help from the bullpen.

The series now went back to Seattle, where once again, Lou Piniella would have to use Randy Johnson on only three days' rest — his fifth outing in only sixteen days. Could the exhausted Johnson get up to full form?

Tired, arm-weary, and lacking his great fastball, Johnson allowed four runs over seven and a third innings. Not bad, but not good enough. The Indians' Dennis Martinez was magnificent, shutting the Mariners out, 4–0, to end Seattle's magnificent run. It was all over.

The Mariners had had their greatest season. They had riveted fans all across the country, bringing them back to baseball after they'd been angered by the players' strike.

Ken Griffey Jr., in spite of the injury that had caused him to miss half the season, had led his team to the third-greatest comeback in major league history and had tied the record for playoff home runs — all with a metal plate holding his wrist together.

Best of all, he had gotten to the playoffs for the first time. "We'll be back," he promised when it was all over. "This October stuff is fun. I'll get the hang of it."

Chapter Seventeen:
1996–2000

Home Again

After the Mariners' great performance in the 1995 playoffs, enthusiasm for the team was at an all-time high. Plans to build a new ballpark to replace the Kingdome were discussed. Seattle was so loaded with star players that fans didn't doubt the team would make postseason play again. It seemed just a matter of time before they would reach the World Series.

In the off-season, the Mariners rewarded Griffey with a new four-year $36 million contract. Unfortunately, however, after paying Griffey, the Mariners couldn't afford to retain all their other stars. They were forced to trade Tino Martinez and reliever Jeff Nelson to the Yankees and sent Mike Blowers to the Dodgers. Still, with twenty-year-old shortstop Alex Rodriguez ready for the majors, the Mariners looked like one of the strongest clubs in baseball.

Griffey had the metal plate removed from his wrist and looked forward to another spectacular season. But little went right for the Mariners in 1996.

After starting the season 5–0, in May pitcher Randy Johnson went down with a back injury. He didn't win another game for the rest of the season. They also lost new third baseman Russ Davis for the balance of the season after he broke his leg. Then in mid-June Griffey broke a small bone in his right hand and had to have surgery. He was out of the lineup for a month.

Fortunately, Alex Rodriguez picked up the slack with a spectacular season, leading the league with 141 runs, 54 doubles, and a .358 batting average. The Mariners were close to division-leading Texas when Griffey returned in mid-July.

But the Mariner pitching staff simply couldn't do the job without Randy Johnson. Texas edged them out for the division title by 4½ games, and Baltimore nipped the Mariners for the wild card spot.

Despite missing 25 games with the injury to his hand, Griffey still belted 49 home runs, third in the league behind Mark McGwire's 52 for Oakland and Brady Anderson's 50 for Baltimore. Had he not been injured, Griffey very well may have broken Roger Maris's all-time single-season record of 61. Entering the 1997 season, baseball fans around the country looked forward to watching Griffey go for the record. And with Johnson healthy, Mariner fans looked forward to the postseason once again. Most observers picked them to win the American League pennant.

Both Johnson and Griffey got off to a quick start. Johnson won his first start and Griffey was the American League Player of the Week after cracking 6 homers in the first eight games of the season. They surged to the lead in the Western Division.

Their power-packed lineup produced runs in bunches. Jamie Moyer and Jeff Fassero emerged to give the Mariners two solid starting pitchers behind Johnson. But the three players couldn't pitch every inning, and the Seattle bullpen kept blowing leads.

It was thanks to Griffey that the Mariners stayed on top. His 13 April home runs set a record, and by the end of May he'd cracked a total of 24. Maris's record seemed well within reach.

The team made several mid-season trades, sending their best prospects to other teams to shore up the pitching staff. The club was gambling with the future but thought a stronger bullpen could get them to the World Series. Fans began to anticipate both a world championship for the Mariners and a new home run record for Ken Griffey.

Both would prove hard to come by. In late June Griffey went into an apparently inexplicable power drought. Over the next month he hit only a handful of home runs, effectively putting Maris's record out of reach. Although he continued to get hits and drive in runs, home runs were suddenly scarce.

No one knew it at the time, but Griffey's home run slump coincided with the death of his mother-in-law. As he explained later, "I have a three-year-old son, and I had to tell him he was never going to see his grandmother again. It was tough."

When Griffey got hot again in late July, the Mariners took command of the division race and finished six games ahead of the second-place Angels. Griffey had been spectacular, hitting 56 homers. As a team, the Mariners set a new major-league record by bopping 264 home runs. In the divisional playoff series, they faced Baltimore.

Everyone expected the Mariners to outslug the

Orioles, and it didn't seem possible that Randy Johnson, who went 20–4 during the regular season, could be beat. But Mariner bats went silent in the series, including Griffey's. He managed only 2 hits and 2 RBIs. And while Johnson pitched well, Seattle's bullpen fell apart, and the Mariners lost three games to one.

The pain of the Mariners' loss was lessened somewhat for Griffey in the off-season when he was unanimously selected as the American League's Most Valuable Player, only the ninth such selection in league history. "When you look at what Junior's done and the skills he possesses," said manager Lou Piniella, "you have to say that he's as good as anyone who's played." For Griffey, individual honors were nice, but winning a World Series still remained his goal. If the Mariners could only solve their bullpen problems, that still seemed within reach.

But in 1998 the Mariners seemed to come unglued. Their pitching collapsed completely, as even Randy Johnson struggled, and the club fought to maintain a .500 record. For many fans, however, Ken Griffey filled the void.

He got off to another fast start, hitting his 300th

career home run in April to become the second-youngest player ever to reach that mark. Before the season was a month old, everyone was talking about the possibility that Roger Maris's home run record would be broken. Only this season Griffey had some competition.

St. Louis first baseman Mark McGwire also started off strong. Over the first few months of the season, Griffey and McGwire matched each other home run for home run. By the middle of the season, each man had almost 40 home runs!

The pressure on each player was intense, as the press followed each and every at-bat closely. By the All-Star Game, Griffey was beginning to show the effects of the pressure. He grew tired of being asked the same questions every day, and with the Mariners struggling, he didn't seem to be having as much fun as he once did.

At the All-Star break, he angered fans when he announced that he wasn't going to participate in the annual home run hitting contest held the day before the game. As Griffey explained, he was swinging the bat well and "I'm afraid it might mess up my swing." He was shocked at the response to his announcement.

Overnight, some fans turned against him, calling him selfish.

He was sensitive to the criticism and finally decided to participate in the contest, which fans hoped would be a chance to see him go head-to-head with Mark McGwire in the finals. But McGwire was eliminated early. With a series of long home runs, Griffey won the contest going away.

But even that proved to be controversial. In interviews both before and after the contest, he seemed distracted and unhappy. Fans were puzzled by the fact that he seemed to take little joy from the game he had always loved.

There were many reasons for his change in attitude. His team wasn't doing well and he was uncomfortable with all the attention he was receiving. But he was also the target of some unconscionable behavior by some fans.

McGwire was white, and some narrow-minded fans didn't want an African American player to break Maris's record. They had made their feelings known to Griffey both through the mail and at the ballpark. That bothered Griffey and caused him to become withdrawn. He began keeping his feelings to himself.

Still, he managed to keep pace with McGwire into August. Then his home run pace slowed, and Sammy Sosa took over as McGwire's main challenger. Attention turned away from Griffey as both Sosa and McGwire shattered Maris's mark. McGwire finally finished with 72 home runs, while Sosa hit 66 and led the Chicago Cubs into the playoffs. Griffey, meanwhile, wound up with "only" 56 home runs as the Mariners finished a disappointing third in the Western Division, with a record of 76–85.

He was happy when the season ended and he was able to spend time with his family again. They had moved to Florida, where they lived in a beautiful house in the same neighborhood as Tiger Woods, with whom Griffey became good friends. It made him sad when he had to leave his family to attend spring training in Arizona.

For the first time in years, no one expected the Mariners to be a playoff team. Randy Johnson's contract was due to expire, and he had made it clear that he didn't want to re-sign with the club. So he had been traded to Houston late in the 1998 season. Without Johnson, the Mariners didn't have anyone on the pitching staff they could count on. Cost overruns on their new ballpark, Safeco Field, had left the organization with little money to spend on new players, so the team wouldn't be able to replace him.

Already fans were wondering if the Mariners could afford to keep both Griffey and Alex Rodriguez, both of whom would be due new contracts after the 2000 season. There was plenty of speculation that one of the two stars would eventually be traded.

In the first half of the 1999 season, both the Mariners and Griffey performed up to expectations — the Mariners weren't very good, and no matter how well Griffey played, it wasn't enough for the fans. Even after he was named to Major League Baseball's All-Century Team, he was still the object of criticism in Seattle.

In mid-season the franchise got a shot in the arm when the ballclub moved into Safeco Field. Unlike the dreary Kingdome, the new ballpark was a beautiful open-air stadium with a grass field and a roof that could be closed to keep the rain out yet not fully enclose the park. It is unlike any other ballpark in baseball.

Although Griffey liked being able to play outdoors, he was disappointed in the park's dimensions. Tired of giving up too many runs, the Mariners had made their new park a so-called pitcher's park, with dimensions much bigger than the Kingdome. Griffey knew it would be difficult for him to hit home runs there.

His fears were proved correct over the last half of the season. He hit fly ball after fly ball that would have been a home run in the Kingdome. But at Safeco, they came to earth on the warning track for outs. At one point he was overheard screaming in frustration at Seattle general manager Woody Woodward, "Get me out of this place! Trade me right now!" After cracking 56 in each of the previous two seasons, his season total of 48 home runs was a disappointment.

At the end of the season Griffey had only one year remaining on his contract. The Mariners wanted to sign him to a new one but knew that if they were unable to, Griffey would have to be traded.

They had already offered him an amazing eight-year deal worth $138 million, but Griffey had rejected the proposal. That winter, the Mariners began entertaining offers for their star.

According to baseball rules, Griffey had the right to reject any trade because he was a veteran of more than ten years, including five with the same team. He gave the Mariners a short list of clubs he would be willing to be traded to.

Top on his list were the Cincinnati Reds. Not only was Cincinnati his hometown, but his father was now a coach for the Reds, and the Reds were coming off a 96-win season. They seemed a lot closer to reaching the World Series than were the Mariners. In addition, playing in Cincinnati would make it easier for Griffey to spend time with his wife and children. Florida was a six-hour flight from Seattle but only two hours from Cincinnati, and the Reds held spring training near his Florida home.

The Reds and Mariners dickered back and forth for weeks. The Reds wanted him, but they couldn't afford to match Seattle's contract offer. Griffey told them he would be willing to take less money for the opportunity to play for the Reds. As he later explained, "I can't spend the money I have now. You don't want to go to a team that has half of its budget all in one player. We're in this together."

Finally, the Mariners accepted Cincinnati's offer, which gave them outfielder Mike Cameron, pitcher Brett Tomko, and some prospects for Griffey. The Reds immediately signed Griffey to a nine-year deal for $116.5 million. "Every little boy has a dream of playing at home in front of his friends and family, and it was the same with me," he said. Ken Griffey was going back home.

Reds fans were thrilled and before the season bought tickets in record numbers. They looked forward to seeing Griffey on the same field with long-time star Barry Larkin and two of the game's most exciting young players, second baseman Pokey Reese and first baseman Sean Casey. After winning 96 games in 1999, they expected Griffey to lead them to a world championship in 2000.

But it was not to be. As happy as he was to be playing in Cincinnati, Griffey and the Reds got off to an uncharacteristically slow start. At the beginning of June, Griffey's average was just over .200 and the Reds were barely a .500 team.

Scheduled to move into a new ballpark in 2003,

Reds management apparently gave up on the season and began planning for the future, trading their best pitcher, Denny Neagle, to the Yankees. Griffey was disappointed to be part of a rebuilding program, yet over the second half of the season, despite suffering from some nagging injuries, he rebounded. By the end of the year he had pulled his average back up to a respectable .271 and hit 40 home runs with 118 RBIs, both club highs. And the Reds played surprisingly well in the second half, demonstrating that the near future might not be so bad after all.

The player they once called "the Kid" and "Junior" has grown up, and it looks as if baseball is beginning to be fun for him again. "Hopefully," he said just before the end of the season, "I can have the same luck my dad did," referring to his father's two World Series rings.

"That's why I play this game."

Matt Christopher®

Lance Armstrong	Michael Jordan
Kobe Bryant	Mario Lemieux
Terrell Davis	Tara Lipinski
Julie Foudy	Mark McGwire
Jeff Gordon	Greg Maddux
Wayne Gretzky	Hakeem Olajuwon
Ken Griffey Jr.	Shaquille O'Neal
Mia Hamm	Alex Rodriguez
Tony Hawk	Briana Scurry
Grant Hill	Sammy Sosa
Ichiro	Venus and Serena Williams
Derek Jeter	Tiger Woods
Randy Johnson	Steve Young

The #1 Sports Series for Kids

Matt CHRISTOPHER®

Read them all!

*Previously published as *Crackerjack Halfback*

All available in paperback from Little, Brown and Company